The Language of Sculpture

THE LANGUAGE OF SCULPTURE

WILLIAM TUCKER

with 155 illustrations

THAMES AND HUDSON

© 1974 Thames and Hudson Ltd, London
First paperback edition 1977
Reprinted 1988

Filmset and printed in Great Britain by
BAS Printers Limited, Over Wallop, Hampshire

Contents

Preface

This book started as a series of lectures, on Picasso, Brancusi, Matisse and David Smith, given at the University of Leeds during my period there as Gregory Fellow in Sculpture. The lectures were subsequently published, under the general title 'Four Sculptors', in *Studio International* from April 1970. The chapter on González was originally commissioned for the catalogue to the 1970 Tate Gallery exhibition, but was not used because of objections from the artist's family. The chapters 'Rodin', 'Brancusi at Tîrgu Jiu', 'The Object' and 'Gravity' were published in *Studio International* from October 1972.

The original preface to the book concluded with the comment that it was written 'from the perspective of a sculptor working now, rather than that of the historian, critic or connoisseur'. Some twenty years have passed since I started work on the lectures on which the book was based; my perspective has changed radically as my sculpture has moved in a direction I could hardly have anticipated in the late 1960s. Yet if I were to rewrite these essays today, I think the changes would be of emphasis, rather than substance.

I would like to remember the advice and help given me by sculptor friends in London when working on the material for the book, and especially of Sidney Geist, another sculptor-writer, whose contribution to our understanding of Brancusi remains unequalled.

Poetry is the subject of the poem,
From this the poem issues and
To this returns.

WALLACE STEVENS
The Man with the Blue Guitar, XXII

Introduction

'Sculpture was a separate thing, as was the easel picture, but it did not require a wall like the picture. It did not even need a roof. It was an object that could exist for itself alone, and it was well to give it entirely the character of a complete thing about which one could walk, and which one could look at from all sides. And yet it had to distinguish itself somehow from other things, the ordinary things which everyone could touch. It had to become un-impeachable, sacrosanct, separated from chance and time through which it rose isolated and miraculous, like the face of a seer. It had to be given its own certain place, in which no arbitrariness had placed it, and it must be inter-calated in the silent continuance of space and its great laws. It had to be fitted into the space that surrounded it, as into a niche; its certainty, steadiness and loftiness did not spring from its significance but from its harmonious adjust-ment to the environment.'[1]

Thus the German poet R. M. Rilke, in his monograph on Rodin, written in 1903. Rilke was 28 and had arrived in Paris the previous year, though he had for some time been familiar with Rodin's work. The experience of Rodin's sculpture was crucial to the development of his poetic thought: and while his essay remains the outstanding interpretation of Rodin's œuvre, anticipating and rendering otiose almost all subsequent criticism, it contains much also that pre-figures the development of sculpture after Rodin. Rilke's concept of sculpture as essentially object is not one which today would seem to characterize the work of Rodin. Yet Rilke, pressing in his own thought towards the work of art as 'thing', *Kunstding* rather than *Kunstwerk*, in the world but not of it, 'isolated from the spectator as though by a non-conduct-ing vacuum',[2] projected this idea into the sculpture of Rodin, where it was latent, the work for which it was most apt, that of Brancusi, not yet having come into existence. Indeed, during the year 1903, Brancusi was making a solitary journey across Europe, much of it on foot, towards Paris.[3] Julio González was already in Paris, and Picasso was to settle there permanently in the following year. Matisse in 1903 completed *The Serf*, after three years' application – a labour miraculously belied by the vigour of the conception, the urgency of the handling. Rilke, in his vision of sculpture as the necessary

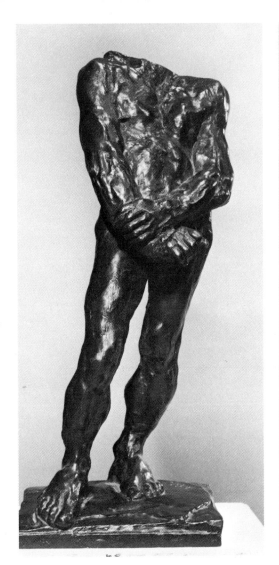

1 AUGUSTE RODIN *Nude Balzac Study F c.* 1896

2 EDGAR DEGAS *Dancer Fastening the String of her Tights* 1882–95

art for this moment in history, with its concreteness both as object and as process, its compound existence in everyday reality and in the inner world of the imagination, belonged to the generation of younger men who were searching for a way past the giant figure of Rodin.

Rodin himself was at that time approaching the height of his fame, his pre-eminence confirmed, both among artists and the public at large, by the scandal over the Balzac monument in the late 1890s, and by his great retrospective exhibition at the Exposition Universelle of 1900. In contrast, his contemporary Degas, who had abandoned first oil painting and then pastel,

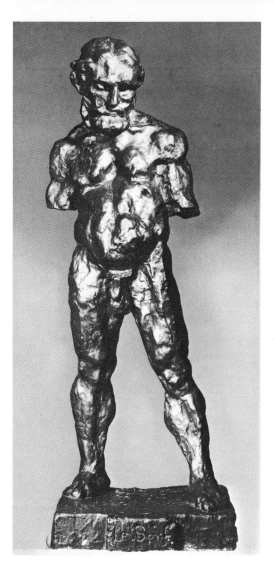

3 Henri Matisse *The Serf* 1900–03

4 Constantin Brancusi *The Prayer* 1907

to devote himself wholly to sculpture, was working in total obscurity: his life's work in sculpture was revealed only in 1921, with the exhibition of bronzes cast from the wax models found in his studio after his death four years earlier. The originality and authority of his work – equalling, even exceeding that of Rodin – yielded itself as gradually as Rodin's impact was immediate.

To appreciate the profound re-orientation of sensibility implied in Rilke's essay, consider comparable figures by the older sculptors, Rodin and Degas, and the younger men, Matisse and Brancusi: Rodin's headless Balzac study 'F' from the mid-1890s;[4] Degas' *Dancer Fastening the String of her Tights*,[5] probably made slightly earlier; Matisse's *The Serf*; and Brancusi's *The Prayer* of 1907. The similarities are at first perhaps more apparent than the differences: all stand complete and separate, within Rilke's condition, needing neither architecture nor subject-matter as justification, not even needing a title to direct the response of the spectator (the Matisse and Brancusi pieces are perhaps wilfully archaic in this respect). But where the sculptures of the older and younger men fundamentally differ is in this: the *Dancer* and the Balzac study are primarily figures, *The Serf* and *The Prayer* primarily sculptures. However anonymous Degas' figure, however stressed as 'mechanism' (Valéry's term),[6] as a tensed and balanced construct of volumes; however 'abstract' the Balzac study, with its richly expressive surface, braced limbs and great axial thrust; still these abstract components serve to affirm our experience of the sculpture as figure, as essentially our own physical structure realized outside ourselves. *The Serf* and *The Prayer*, on the other hand, are 'things in themselves': in Matisse's much-used expression, 'architecture'. They are thematically, but not expressively, figures. The 'musculature' of *The Serf*, seen against that of the Balzac study, reveals itself as a discontinuous and arbitrary array of lumps more suggestive of vegetable life than human anatomy. The great sweep, the hidden but utterly convincing coherence of internal structure, the broad and rhythmic connection and disposition of mass, which are characteristic of Rodin's Balzac study – and which, as *Madeleine I* and paintings of the same model used for *The Serf* demonstrate, were well within Matisse's grasp at this time – are expressly sacrificed to the naïve immediacy of perception attendant on a traditional and neutral subject, and to a consequent and even greater innocence and directness in the handling of material. The proportions, the balance, the distribution of weight in the figure, are as deliberately unconvincing as its discontinuous structure. It is the very antithesis of Rodin, with his sculptor's tricks and his artfulness: it is clearly the child of Cézanne rather than of Rodin, the first fruit of a lifelong and heroic struggle to make sculpture structured not by anatomy or some imposed expressive purpose, but by the willed coherence of perception alone.

Brancusi's *The Prayer* is a sculptor's sculpture, and reveals its originality with discretion. As a figure it is as graceless as *The Serf*, more so perhaps, because the female form creates expectations of this quality that are stretched but by no means absent in Degas. *The Prayer* is fundamentally a geometric structure, an organization of volumes that moves beyond *The Serf* in the reconstruction of the human figure in the interests of an order particular to the individual object: an order which was to be more directly and economically achieved, later in the same year (1907), in the rectangular limestone block from which the first *Kiss* was carved. In both sculptures the clear and strong design of the whole sculpture is brought back towards the human by subtlety and delicacy of touch in details of modelling and articulation. If *The Serf* is the first modern sculpture, *The Kiss* is the first fully achieved sculpture-object, fulfilling all the terms which Rilke had set out for the art which he correctly credited Rodin with rescuing, forty years before, from the degradation of 'the superficial, cheap and comfortable metier'[7] of nineteenth-century Salon sculpture.

5 CONSTANTIN BRANCUSI *The Kiss* 1907

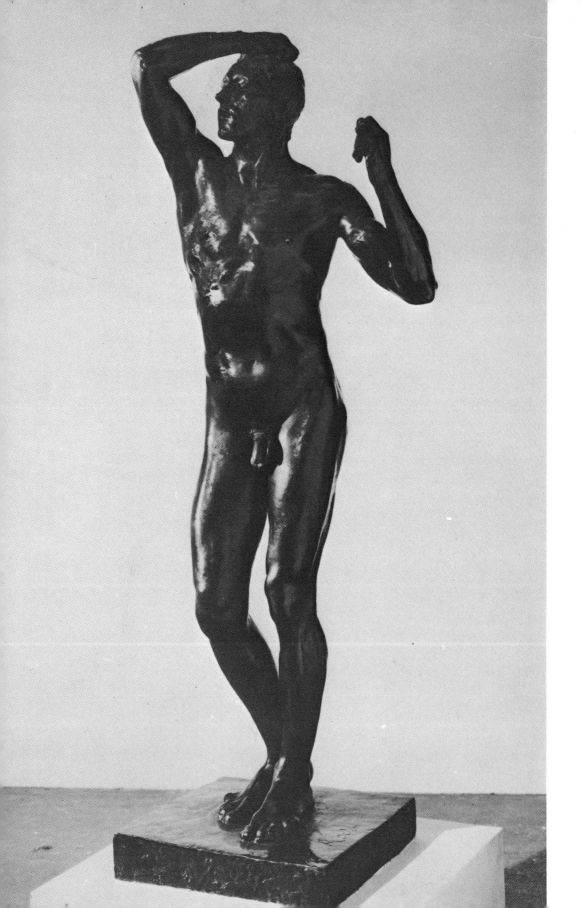

1 Rodin

Auguste Rodin was born in Paris in 1840, in the same year as Monet, Renoir and Sisley. Cézanne was born the year before; Degas in 1834, Manet in 1832, and Pissarro in 1830.[1] Rodin was thus the exact or virtual contemporary of each of the painters whose work emerged during the 1860s as the prototype of modernism. By 1877, the year in which Rodin completed his first major sculpture to be accepted by the Salon, *The Age of Bronze*, the Impressionists were already holding their third group exhibition. Rodin's sculpture began to appear at the time when the Impressionists had already established not only their public presence (they were still far from commercial success) but also the fundamental and radical principles of their art. Thus Rodin's mature sculpture follows the effective emergence of modern painting; moreover, in comparison with the directness, simplicity and objectivity of the new painting, the statement in sculpture seems tentative, half-formed and weighed down by a burden of Romantic and dramatic subject-matter, of moral and public 'function', which the Impressionists had been able to jettison from the first.[2]

The reasons for the late arrival and confused intentions of the new sculpture lie partly in the physical character of sculpture and painting, partly in their relative development in Europe since the Renaissance, partly in the specific conditions of patronage and public taste which obtained in nineteenth-century France: but most importantly in the existence of a radical tradition in French painting since the neo-classicism of David had been adopted as the official art of the Revolution. A number of the most talented and ambitious artists of the century, including Delacroix, Corot, Courbet, Rousseau, Boudin, Jongkind and the Barbizon painters, had prepared the ground for the Impressionists, and in some cases were still at hand to advise and encourage the younger men at the outset of their careers. Though Géricault, Préault, Daumier, all made sculpture that is now retrospectively claimed as the forerunner of modernism, their 'pioneer' work was at the time unknown or not taken seriously *as sculpture*.

Only Carpeaux, whose *Dance* for the Paris Opera engaged the antagonism of the Academy in 1868, can fairly be claimed to have played the same kind

6 AUGUSTE RODIN *The Age of Bronze* 1877

of role for sculpture, as, say, Courbet for painting; Carpeaux in fact taught Rodin briefly at the Petite Ecole, but had no further connection with him before his early death in 1875.

This is not to say that Rodin, once established, lacked encouragement from older artists: in fact, from the controversy over *The Age of Bronze* onwards, he found a support from some members of the Academy and influential public officials which probably exceeded that given to the Impressionists at the time. Because of the traditional elements which persisted in his sculpture, and the controversies aroused by the commissioned monuments, Rodin's public reputation soon overhauled that of his radical contemporaries in painting, until by 1900 he was probably the most famous artist in the world. By contrast, the later and profoundly important developments in the careers of the Impressionist painters, in Cézanne, in Monet and in the sculpture of Degas, took place well out of the public eye.

Today we are only beginning to disentangle the various strands in the art of Rodin: to extract what is distinctively modern from the confusion and rhetoric with which both an impoverished tradition and too great a commercial and public success encumbered it. What is intrinsic in Rodin to the development of modern sculpture – the independence of the work from specific subject-matter or function, its 'internal' life, the concern with material, structure, and gravity as ends in themselves – these elements have to be elucidated, for they are clearly there; but this must be done without special pleading, and with a full awareness of the historical conditions under which his art emerged.

If one compares Rodin's early years with those of his immediate contemporaries, Monet, Renoir and Cézanne, significant distinctions emerge which spring not only from individual background and temperament but from the wholly different opportunities which sculpture and painting, respectively, offered to a young artist of ambition in the 1850s. The paths through which a specifically modern idiom could be channelled were manifestly quite different in the two arts. As a result of his father's limited means (he was employed as a clerk in a government department) and his own apparent incapacity to learn anything at school, Rodin was allowed at the age of fourteen to enter the free Petite Ecole to do the one thing that interested him, drawing. At this school he discovered the modelling class – 'For the first time I saw artists' clay; I thought I had gone to Heaven', he said later – and decided on the instant that he would become a sculptor.[3] By the age of 17 he had applied to, and been rejected by, the 'Grande Ecole', the Ecole des Beaux-Arts, three times. For the next 20 years Rodin had to make a living as a craftsman and assistant, notably to Carrier-Belleuse, the most successful academic-commercial sculptor of the period, while continuing his private apprenticeship in art in his own time.

In his reading, his ambition – confirmed by a visit to Rome and Florence in 1875 – his handling of clay and his treatment of the figure, he was thus virtually self-educated. His contacts were with fellow craftsmen and academic 'superiors'; the two older sculptors of talent and independence whose classes he attended, Barye and Carpeaux, had no exchange with him. *The Age of Bronze* in the Salon in 1877 caused a sensation not only for its evident internal qualities, its challenge to everything the Academy stood for, but because it was a sculpture apparently without antecedent, by an artist whose preparation for envisaged greatness, for a new role for sculpture itself, had been utterly private, isolated and obscure.

Nineteenth-century sculpture was wholly unprepared to sustain any serious aesthetic purpose: all the great issues that had torn painting apart – the choice between Ingres and Delacroix and between colour and line; the realism of Millet and Courbet; the rise of pure landscape – had left sculpture untouched. Extreme Romanticism in sculpture was simply ignored in the prolonged exclusion of Préault from the Salon. Much of what must seem diffuse or rhetorical in Rodin's subsequent ambition and subject-matter derives from his attempt to include in the repertory of sculpture themes long exhausted in painting. In terms of a newly conceived independence for sculpture, Rodin must be Géricault, Delacroix and Courbet simultaneously with Manet and Cézanne.

The contrast with the earlier years of the Impressionists is remarkable. Most of the group came from middle-class, even well-to-do, families. Only Renoir had a similar background to Rodin; but none had the rigorous craft apprenticeship from an early age, or experienced the bitterness of repeated rejection by the Beaux-Arts. All the important members of the group, except Pissarro and Cézanne, studied at the Beaux-Arts; all were from an early date acquainted with other young men with similar aims and ambitions in art and with radical artists of an earlier generation.

During the two decades when Rodin was earning a solitary living as a craftsman and producing little personal work of substance, his contemporaries in painting developed a common ambition and purpose in the presentation of a new vision, a new idea, and produced a great number of fine and personal paintings, including several masterpieces; which is not to deny that Monet, Pissarro and Renoir suffered hardship and poverty equal to Rodin's in this period; and all endured a similar humiliation and ridicule at the Salon. But whatever their physical privations the painters at least enjoyed the sense of a common enterprise, a new attitude to nature repeatedly realized in achieved paintings of variety and ambition.

Rodin could have no such satisfaction; it was simply not in the nature of sculpture as an art to achieve the immediacy, the directness of realization, of Impressionist painting. The ideal of objectivity, of truth to sensation – and the

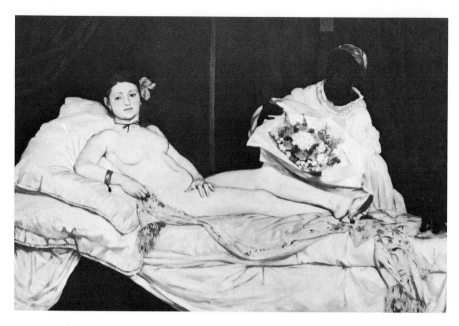

7 EDOUARD MANET *Olympia* 1863

necessity to work in the open air and at great speed without correction or re-working – gave painting a flexibility it has not enjoyed before or since. That kind of directness could be achieved in sculpture only through an enormous and expensive preliminary effort of organization, unthinkable without the backing of a substantial commission, for which this kind of expression would likely prove quite unsuitable. Never have the physical natures of painting or sculpture stood in greater contrast than at this period: painting functioning with a maximum of economy, with the richest effects issuing from the simplest of means; sculpture, apparently doomed to complete impotence by the complexity and inertia of the medium itself. For all the newness of the perceptual basis of Monet's and Renoir's painting, and of their handling of paint and use of colour, they depended ultimately on an established language of painting that had emerged about three centuries previously. It was the optical, technical and economic innovations of the Renaissance that made possible the easel painting in oils, given by perspective a satisfying and homogeneous illusion of depth and volume. The inability of Renaissance sculpture to capture space and atmosphere – to say nothing of the obvious physical problems of making, handling and disposing of masses of bronze and stone – precluded sculpture, from Michelangelo onwards, as an art in which a substantial dialogue between the personal vision of the artist and the common components of the medium could function. Sculpture became an art in which the taste and ambition of the public patron became the determining factor, and virtuosity and craftsmanship the criterion of artistic achievement. The academic sculpture of the nineteenth century, with its appalling virtuosity, the vulgarity of its subject-matter, its total lack of real feeling, intelligence or sensitivity, was as much the prisoner of conditions established centuries earlier as Impressionism was the final and convulsive gesture of liberation in a continuous and parallel tradition, which had expanded and enriched itself as its companion had degenerated.

If one must choose one in particular of his contemporaries in painting to compare with Rodin, I would favour Manet. His *Olympia* at the Salon of 1865 anticipated the impact of *The Age of Bronze* some twelve years later: the general components and ambitions of both works relate. Both are based on Renaissance models, but the physical types depicted seemed aggressively actual and uncomfortably 'real'; most importantly, both works are characterized by a freedom of handling, a studied and skilful response to the qualities of the medium – brushed oil paint on a flat rectangle, clay literally *handled*, modelled with equal feeling and intensity throughout the figure. From here on, the differences become more significant than the similarities, but the main point of comparison between Rodin and the Impressionists is established, *not* in the realization of light, as is sometimes stated – it was necessary to await Brancusi for a comparable achievement in sculpture – but in the affirmation of *surface*, of the perceptible physicality of the medium.

This single common preoccupation has a special significance, moreover: it represents the point at which illusioned space in sculpture and its counterpart in painting coincided, as both arts travelled in opposite directions. Just as the affirmation of surface in Monet, by clearly perceptible brushmarks of equal emphasis, goes far to eliminate the illusion of deep space persisting from Renaissance perspective, so the affirmation of surface in Rodin, of clay felt and handled for itself, as material, signifies the beginning of the release of structure from subject, the articulation of an illusioned envelope of space created by the animation of the surface, independent of the traditional illusion of 'life' of the figure.

In discussions of Rodin's modernity, the emphasis on his modelling, his use of clay, has correctly, in my view, been the dominant feature. But there is perhaps a tendency to see in his modelling a renewal of possibly long-forgotten traditional usage, rather than what it really is, a total and violent break with the past, achieved through the uninhibited manipulation of substance to the point at which the intelligible communication of form would break down, were it not for the figure as vehicle. Clay is here asserted for what it is: soft, inert, structureless, essentially passive, taking form from the action of the hands and fingers; however rich in potential, especially in response to the resource, talent and training of Rodin, it remains one material among many. The first materials of modern sculpture – clay in the hands of Rodin, carved stone and wood in the hands of Brancusi – were the traditional materials, but felt and used as if for the first time.

Of the originality of Rodin's handling of clay, there can be no question. It is true that bronze was the material of 'Romantic' sculpture before Rodin, notably in the hands of Barye and Préault, and of the most vigorous public monuments – such as Rude's *Marseillaise* and *Marshal Ney*; that sculptors had for centuries produced small sketch models in clay that are sometimes remarkably free; and that Carpeaux had carried over this freedom of surface into larger-scale work, a deliberate challenge to academic conceptions of finish. But if one compares, for example, the celebrated clay sketch models of Canova, the feeling is utterly different: in Canova the surface is brittle, torn, ragged, gouged-out, but, however loose, it remains a surface, a skin. In Rodin one senses the identity of external event with internal force: clay is

8 ANTONIO CANOVA *Study for Cupid and Psyche* 1793

9 AUGUSTE RODIN *Mask of the Man with the Broken Nose* 1864

10 AUGUSTE RODIN *The Man with the Broken Nose* 1872

felt as substance, not *over* the surface, but *through* every cubic inch of volume. Rilke describes how Rodin discovered 'the fundamental element of his art; as it were, the germ of his world. It was the surface – this differently great surface, variedly accentuated, accurately measured, out of which everything must rise – which was from this moment the subject-matter of his art. . . . His art was not built upon a great idea, but upon a minute, conscientious realization, upon the attainable, upon a craft.'[4]

The Man with the Broken Nose, modelled when Rodin was only twenty-three, embodies the core of his originality, before his exposure to Michelangelo and Donatello, and before any possible awareness of what was happening in painting. 'There were no symmetrical planes in this face at all, nothing repeated itself, no spot remained empty, dumb or indifferent'.[5]

In spite of the purity and intensity of plastic purpose first noted by Rilke, it is rather the distractions, the incoherence, the overstatement of Rodin's work, taken as a whole, that must strike us today. It is heavy with the nineteenth century, in contrast to the stripped and private commitment of Degas

21

in sculpture, which grew in solitude, as Rodin's grew in public, during exactly the same period – the twenty-five-odd years from 1880.

What Rodin and Degas importantly have in common is the rediscovery of *volume* as the fundamental consideration in sculpture: Rodin determined by his 'contours'[6] to realize the animation of the sculpture from every view, in reaction against the 'bas-relief' compositional procedures of his academic contemporaries; Degas searching for a more convincing and satisfying 'truth', in the volumetric reconstruction of the figure in sculpture, than could ever be afforded by single-point perspective on the plane surface.

It is too easy to explain away the prolixity and diversity of Rodin's work, and the confusions of his conception of the role of sculpture, by looking back to four centuries of neglect, and assuming that he somehow felt obliged to make up lost ground by re-invigorating all the conventional modes of sculpture that had atrophied or fallen into decadence. Daumier, Degas and Medardo Rosso found no difficulty in concentrating the aims and sharpening the focus of sculpture in the nineteenth century. Nor will it do to lift out isolated works from the œuvre – such as, notoriously, *The Walking Man*, the fragmented figures of 1890–91, the late *Dancers* – and, on the basis of hindsight and recent taste, proclaim Rodin's modernity in the face of the evidence of the mass of the work.

It is a partial answer to say that, in view of the economics of sculpture, an artist of Rodin's ambition had no alternative but to work through the existing system of the Salon and the public commissions. Yet, having started on this path, why did Rodin stick to it? After the State purchase of the *John the Baptist* and the commission for the *Gates of Hell*, he had effectively gained independence for a radical sculpture on a large scale without reference to public or academic convention. Yet the *Burghers of Calais*, the *Victor Hugo*, the *Balzac*, and the other variously unrealized and frustrated public commissions – to say nothing of the portrait busts and the quantity of *Cupids and Psyches*, *Danaids*, *Brothers and Sisters* and other Salon subjects – indicate a continuing commitment to the conventions of nineteenth-century sculpture. Rodin was dependent on these norms, and measured his ambitions against them; the uncertainty which surrounds the dating of, for example, *The Walking Man*[7] reflects Rodin's own uncertainty about the nature, the status, of the sculpture.

This work, like the *Flying Figure*, the large *Head of Iris* and other pieces now much admired, had no place in the public repertoire of the sculpture of the time: they were the by-product of public commissions, but were only publicly exhibited, if at all in Rodin's lifetime, years after their making. Their home was in his studio, which became over the years, an alternative public theatre in which new work could be appraised by a more informed and more sympathetic audience than the Salon and thus the general public could provide. In studio conditions, it was the work in progress, the unfinished, the fragmentary, that engaged the spectator's attention, and challenged the advanced taste of the time.[8]

By comparison with this duplication of objectives, the sculpture of Daumier and Degas has definition and clarity, but it is in a sense a borrowed clarity. Their ambition to make sculpture came out of a tendency in their work in two dimensions, which increasingly called for a sculptural realization. They effectively used the language of painting to define the role of sculpture.

The problem is coming to look like this: expectations of originality in sculpture were and still are conditioned by our experience of painting, not surprisingly since it has been the dominant art since the Renaissance. Rodin resisted these expectations by reaching out for an as-yet undefined *language of sculpture*: which however he could define for himself only in terms of the conventions, however degraded, of nineteenth-century sculpture: the ambitions of Michelangelo and Donatello; the ideas that informed the late Romantic literature of the period; Naturalism and Symbolism. When talking about his own work, Rodin evades the inherent inconsistencies and contradictions of his stance by continual reference to 'nature' as the touchstone of truth and objectivity in his sculpture, relating himself to those artists in the past – not only Michelangelo, but also the Gothic carvers and recent French sculptors such as Barye and Rude[9] – whom he admired. For Rodin this was possibly the only available tradition he could construct for himself; but we should not take the moral overtones of an avowed attachment to the figure too literally.

It is the way he put the figure to use that is remarkable and distinguishes him from his predecessors. And here Rodin's professed intentions and the physical results part company: Rodin's devotion to 'nature', to truth in representation, results paradoxically in an increasing tendency towards abstraction, as a consequence of the character of the medium and its expressive possibilities.

In the work itself, one can see that Rodin had no reverence for the human figure as such. There is an objectivity, a practicality, about the way in which Rodin set about making sculpture, that clearly marks him off from his academic predecessors and contemporaries. This workmanlike attitude to art is well demonstrated by his advice to Rilke: 'Why don't you just go and look at something – for example an animal in the Jardin des Plantes, and keep on looking at it till you're able to make a poem of it?'[10] Rilke rightly connected Rodin with Cézanne in this respect, the two great 'workers' whose continuous labour and application made possible the great harvest of the modern era.

The *Age of Bronze* is Rodin's prime declaration. Its discovered, worked-for simplicity, balance and clarity challenged the Salon sculptors on their own

11 JOHN GIBSON *The Tinted Venus*
c. 1850

ground; though these were qualities Rodin was subsequently to disown, the sculpture retains a freshness and an authority that depends on its containment of structure and understatement of handling. I still find it more moving than any other sculpture of Rodin's, although it is superficially uncharacteristic. It carries the urgency of the first statement in a new language, based on two fundamental propositions: 1. *The sculptor takes responsibility for every aspect of the work: its conception, its form, its size, its material, its finish, its relation to the spectator.* 2. *The structure of the sculpture is identified with the structure of the figure.*

The first proposition has already been touched on. Rodin's lifelong commitment to clay signalled a total responsibility for the work at every stage, in contrast to the prevailing use of marble by academic sculptors, who thus not only abandoned responsibility for the conception of the work, in terms of a prescribed limitation on subject and form, but also for the final product, which the artist very likely never touched, the transcription into marble being carried out by assistants. The sculptor's role in this process was analogous to that of a modern film director. Academic sculpture by the 1870s had in effect become an industry, commercialized and mechanized to a remarkable extent. The sheer quantity of sculpture produced in the nineteenth century, the degree of craftsmanship, the advances in production methods, were in inverse proportion to creativity, to artistic quality. If one

24

sculpture could be said to have reversed this situation, to have returned the responsibility for sculpture to sculptors, it is the *Age of Bronze*.

The second proposition refers to the economics of form as the first to the economics of process. *The figure is the sculpture, the sculpture is the figure.* Only in face of the *Age of Bronze* can one grasp today now so obvious a conception could for one moment have appeared so liberating. The main formal components of nineteenth-century Salon sculpture were a diluted classicism of composition coupled with a pedantic naturalism of surface and detail. The impact of the *Age of Bronze* on eyes habituated to such figures as Gibson's *Tinted Venus* (itself considered daring in its time) must have been tremendous. Here was a sculpture stripped down to its essentials – no accessories, no ornament, no detail, no story, no message. The sculpture is the figure, the figure is the sculpture – Rodin was simultaneously accused of making a sketch rather than a finished sculpture, and of casting from life. The contradictory character of these charges indicates that Rodin had achieved a new and far higher order of naturalism, in terms of an illusion of reality, of the living model, with a sculpture whose surface is, in academic terms, 'unfinished'. Every aspect of the figure is in fact invented, thought-out new. Rodin deliberately rejected the previous 350 years of Western sculpture in choosing Michelangelo's *Dying Slave* as a model for the pose;[11] and his development of the pose in the *Age of Bronze* exposes the flat, languid and

12 MICHELANGELO BUONARROTI
Dying Slave c. 1513

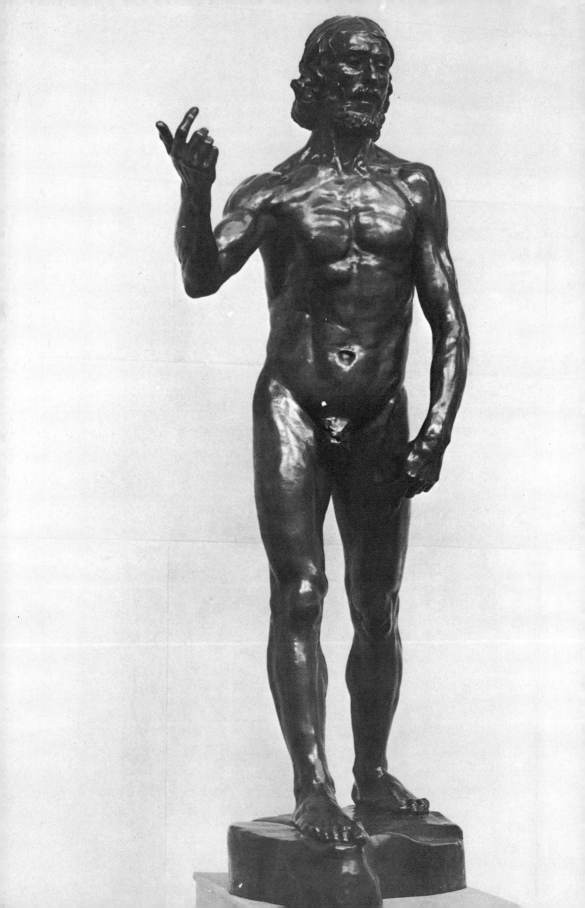

13 Auguste Rodin *St John the Baptist* 1878

14 Auguste Rodin *The Call to Arms* 1878

unconvincing character of the original. But it is the unity of structure with surface that distinguishes the *Age of Bronze* from any earlier sculpture: every inch of the surface is considered, worked on, invented; every inch is equally and differently expressive; expression is diffused from facial expression, from depicted gesture and muscular contortion, into the animation of the entire surface.

In spite of its enormous illusion of life, the sculpture is, then, wholly an invention. This exact coincidence of the abstract and naturalistic is something that had not happened in sculpture since the Renaissance, and the *Age of Bronze* has the character of being made 'out of time'. It was a *tour de force*, and not capable of repetition. Rodin's next three ambitious figure sculptures, *John the Baptist* (1878), *The Call to Arms* (1878) and *Adam* (1880), are by comparison with the *Age of Bronze* vulgar, overstated and confused, and give some indication of the impasse in which Rodin now found himself. He could move towards the frankly naturalistic, eliminating what remained of the graceful

27

15 AUGUSTE RODIN *Adam*
c. 1880

16 AUGUSTE RODIN *The Three Shades* 1880

and idealized in the pose and proportions of the *Age of Bronze*, in favour of the rugged musculature and illusioned movement of *John the Baptist*; or he could increase the freedom and vitality of modelling, but violate the principle of the identity of the sculpture with the figure, as in *The Call to Arms*; or he could move wholly into the Michelangelesque, with the mannered and contorted *Adam*.

Rodin dealt with what he clearly felt to be unresolved in these three sculptures in quite different ways, which separately bear witness to his practicality, the 'making' nature of his effort. *John the Baptist* is by Rodin's own explanation derived from a pose spontaneously taken up by a model; *The Call to Arms* from Rude's *Marseillaise* and Michelangelo's *Pietà*; *Adam* from

the *Pietà* and the Sistine *Creation of Man*;[12] but this dependence is equalled by a respect for what he had made as *component*, the made sculpture becoming both subject and source. Thus the distraction of the over-detailed story-telling head and arms is removed from *John the Baptist* to focus on the illusion of the striding legs of *The Walking Man*; and even the torso has been replaced, with the line of juncture frankly exposed. Abstraction is thus achieved by reduction of the outer limits of the figure. In the case of *Adam*, Rodin abstracts by repetition, arranging three casts of a modified *Adam* as the *Three Shades* in a horizontal sequence on top of the *Gates of Hell*. The absurd proportions and structure of the individual figures are subserved as elements of an intricate and powerful design. The frankness of the use of repetition is unequalled until Brancusi's *Endless Column*. The *Call to Arms*, though no doubt a challenge to the symmetrically heaped, closed pyramid of the academic public monuments, in its vital asymmetry, top-heaviness and agressive penetration of space, nonetheless shares, even exposes, the unconvincing convention of a vertical pile of figures. The horizontal alignment of the *Three Shades* suggested a wholly new solution to the problem of reconciling naturalism with the monumental, which was to find its form in Rodin's first major public commission, *The Burghers of Calais*.

Although 'nature' was and remained Rodin's own touchstone, and the quality of his modelling has been the aspect of his work that has elicited most attention and admiration in this century, both these strands in his sculpture often obscure the fundamental modernity of the work, its character as 'making'. Rodin was primarily concerned with constructing with and within the figure: choosing poses and models from nature; in physically modelling; in the continuous process of casting that went on in his studio as the work proceeded, simultaneously creating a record and new components; in the process of addition or reduction of figures or part-figures until they separately became 'sculpture'. The given structure of the figure, revealed and affirmed by a new freedom in modelling, is used at the same time as the main structural factor internal to the organization of the sculpture, and, externally, as the means of identifying the spectator with the sculpture in terms of his own body responses. The experience of the virtually open-ended commission for the *Gates of Hell* from 1880, in which figures could be assembled and positioned freely without regard to gravity or particular demands of subject-matter, gave Rodin the confidence and freedom to develop this fundamentally abstract constructive direction. For a moment, also, it must have seemed likely to take care of Rodin's perennial problem, that of 'where to finish', as had the exact correspondence of the natural and the invented in the *Age of Bronze*. However, as many of the separate figures from the *Gates* were detached and enlarged as independent sculptures, and as the *Gates* themselves were unfinished at his death thirty-seven years after their inception, the problem had clearly re-presented itself with increased urgency.

Although Rodin claimed to produce slowly, and indeed all his best sculptures until the last period were plainly the fruit of prolonged effort and consideration, a great deal of work emerged from his studio, including many substantial and physically ambitious pieces that were vulgar, facile, unthought-out and pandered to just that Salon taste which he had explicitly challenged with the *Age of Bronze*. Almost all the marbles must come under this criticism, including such monsters as *Eternal Spring* (1884), *The Eternal Idol* (1889), *The Kiss* (1882). It is not surprising that in this category may be found the most popular of Rodin's sculptures. Rodin was here unable or unwilling to alter or modify an initially banal or sentimental conception; the

17 AUGUSTE RODIN *Eternal Spring* 1884

grouping and disposition of the figures is not dictated by hard thought or by the constructive process; and in any case, once the sculpture was in the marble no significant change could take place.

Constructed groupings of existing sculptures from the *Gates*, for example '*I am Beautiful*' and '*Fugit Amor*', are more successful, but the individual components, such as the *Prodigal Son* and the *Crouching Woman*, invariably look much better on their own. With the exception of *The Burghers of Calais*– where the figures are conceived separately and hardly touch, let alone support each other – Rodin's figure groups are bad sculptures: it is not that 'he could not compose', 'had no sense of architecture', etc., but that composition, architecture, structure, could only 'carry' within the limits of the single figure. Multiplication of figures cancels out the distinct expressive potential of each by defining the dramatic too literally, i.e. tying it to a dramatic 'situation', and by sheer visual overstatement.

Both the gravity-free conception of the figures in the *Gates* and the expressively violent nature of the subject-matter opened up new possibilities for structuring the figure. Up to this point, Rodin's figures had been generally upright, self-supporting, the poses derived from classical or Renaissance models, designed to display the expressive performance of an

31

18 Auguste Rodin *Crouching Woman* 1880–82

19 AUGUSTE RODIN *The Prodigal Son* 1889

essentially Renaissance anatomy. With the *Prodigal Son* and the *Crouching Woman*, an entirely new concept of anatomy emerges, in which the human body is re-structured in terms of the posture. Thus, the *Crouching Woman* assumes the compact, closed form of a bunched fist; within it arms and legs, knees and shoulders are torn from their original structural role, their forms and functions deliberately confused in a wilful re-assembly of the body as a bundle of lumps and axes. The *Prodigal Son*, though opposite in its openness and extension, is not so much a kneeling figure as a figure in which the lower legs have been folded back into the horizontal to support its total vertical-diagonal sweep. The sculpture has the character of a single limb, an arm or leg: the proportions and structure of the torso confuse it with leg; the legs and arms penetrate and occupy the body; the arms, with the lower legs removed, also read as legs. In both figures the head is reduced to yet another lump; the neck, if anything, assumes a greater expressive role.

33

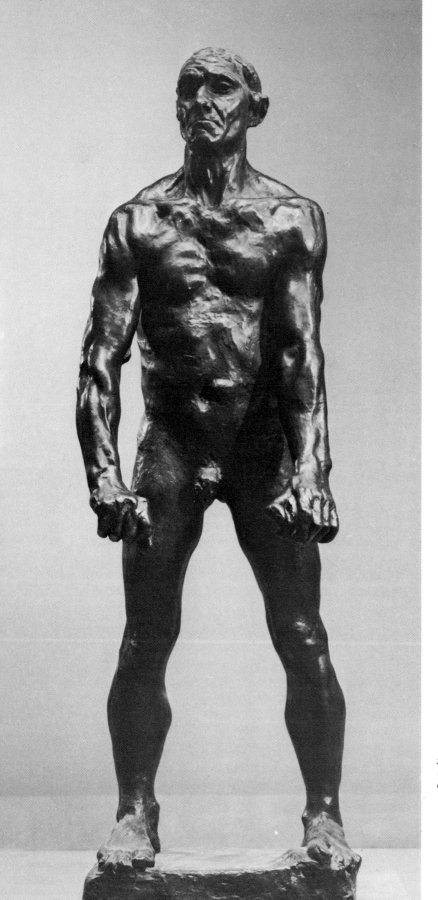

20 AUGUSTE RODIN
Study for Jean d'Aire
c. 1889

21 AUGUSTE RODIN *Torso of Adèle c.* 1882

These two figures were made very shortly after the rhetorical *Adam*, and *The Thinker*, and before the naturalistic *Belle Heaulmière* and the studies for *The Burghers of Calais*. In these sculptures the poses, though far from 'natural', were a good deal more relaxed and static than either the *Gates* or the Michelangelesque pieces. With the over-life-size studies for the *Burghers*, and notably with the gorilla-like *Jean d'Aire*, Rodin took naturalism in terms of the 'lifelike' as far as it can be taken in sculpture. Like the *Age of Bronze*, it is a *tour de force*, and unrepeatable.

The *Torso of Adèle* was made about the same time as the *Prodigal Son* (1882), and is another of the sculptures from the *Gates*. It shares the re-structured anatomy in terms of a unified overall form, this time that of a shallow arch; but the lower legs are simply omitted, and the sculpture is detached from a continuous base. It thus anticipates the great series of partial figures – the *Torso of a Seated Woman Clasping her Left Leg*, the *Flying Figure*, and *Iris, Messenger of the Gods*, of 1890–91, in which some or all of the extremities are omitted – in every case the obtrusive and non-structural head – and no specific orientation is prescribed. These fragments are not arbitrarily or wildly expressive: each sculpture is taut and tightly structured, with the arm or arms bonding to the leg to achieve a constructive unity that can still, by reference to our own body experience, be felt as anatomically 'real'. Of all Rodin's sculptures those in this group probably appeal most to contemporary taste, both through their character as 'objects', by which they were influential on Brancusi and the next generation in Paris, and by their quality of abstract structure, which relates them to the best sculpture being made

35

22 AUGUSTE RODIN *Torso of Seated Woman Clasping her Left Leg c. 1890*

23 AUGUSTE RODIN *Flying Figure* 1890–91

24 AUGUSTE RODIN *Iris,*
Messenger of the Gods 1890–91

today. Yet their abstractness should be taken with caution, for it results from
a desire to express a sense of the figure with increased force: the figure
functions as the vehicle of abstraction. In intention, in feeling, they are
possibly no more abstract than the *Age of Bronze*; they represent a later stage
in Rodin's exploration of the congruent limits of the figure with the sculpture. Although the various stages in this process overlapped – the partial
figure may have started as early as 1877, with *The Walking Man,* and there is
an intense naturalism about several of the *Balzac* studies from the mid-1890s –
nonetheless, if one leaves the major public commissions and the portrait heads
on one side, together with the general mass of enlargements and repeats in
marble that came out of his studio in response to his increasing public success,
one can still observe a succession of attempts to deal with the single figure,
his central theme, to reconcile its dual nature as invented and representational
structure. The succession of these attempts is in the direction of an increasing
abstractness, towards the frank acknowledgment of an *internal, sculptural*
order which evoked rather than represented the figure. The final turn in this
development is revealed in the late small figures of dancers.

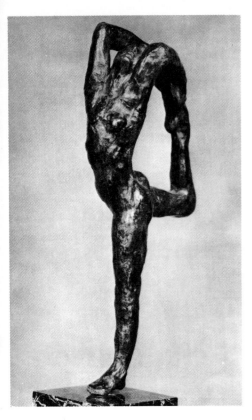

25–28 AUGUSTE RODIN *Dance Movement A-D* c. 1910–11

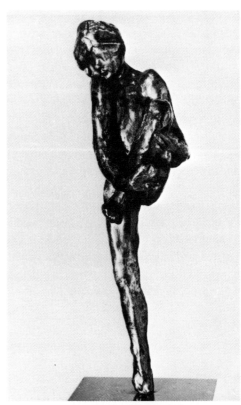

29–32 Auguste Rodin *Dance Movement E-H c.* 1910–11

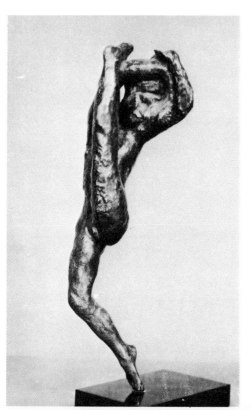

These sculptures, it should be remembered, were made after Brancusi's *Prayer* and *The Kiss* (1907) and Matisse's marvellous trio of sculptures of the same period, the first *Reclining Figure*, the *Serpentine* and the *Two Negresses*, all images of total stability and architectural unity. Rodin's dancers challenge the younger men's work with a totally liberated gestalt, and an even more violent distortion of anatomy in the interest of the representation of abandoned movement. These figures were no sudden invention, but the culmination of a prolonged series of studies, 'improvisations', rapid impressions of movement, which Rodin had made for many years. The whole figure is usually represented, as in the *Prodigal Son*: but the process of re-invention of anatomy in terms of the posture is taken to the point at which the shapes and proportions of the parts defy recognition. The small size of the figures suggests they were made wholly in the sculptor's hand, and they enjoy the freedom of orientation, the identification of the handling of the soft material with structure, that this process allows. It is no longer anatomy but the action of the hand in clay that determines the form of the figure. The idea of 'making' could not be more directly fulfilled.

2 Brancusi:
the Elements of Sculpture

Brancusi was not the first younger sculptor to rebel against Rodin; but when he did, it was with a dedication, a sense of mission, a will to identify his own destiny with that of sculpture itself, that echoed Rodin, together with a grasp of the *essential* qualities of Rodin's achievement, a penetration to the core of Rodin's art, that surpassed the understanding of his contemporaries and enabled him, with progressively increasing confidence, to stand Rodin on his head. Yet the confrontation with Rodin, the deliberate inversion of his vision of sculpture, would have had no weight except in the context of an equal ambition and the development of other, as significant but less apparent, factors in an older tradition which Rodin himself had revived.

Constantin Brancusi was born in 1876 in a village called Hobitza in the part of Romania called Oltenia, then one of the most remote and backward corners of Europe. He had little affection for his family, peasant farmers, and ran away from home twice before leaving finally at the age of eleven. He could neither read nor write until he entered the School of Arts and Crafts at Craiova in 1895. The absence of formal education, the craft apprenticeship, the solitude and independence of the years of childhood and youth, all recall Rodin.

However, in contrast to the decadence of the sculpture tradition in which Rodin had grown up, Brancusi was early exposed to the unpretentious but vigorous qualities both of the general use of wood in his homeland and of a relatively young tradition of realistic sculpture in the Western style, imported to celebrate the heroes of Romania's recent unification and independence. At the Bucharest Academy, which he attended from 1898 to 1902, Brancusi absorbed this tradition of patient, economical and detailed rendering of objective fact, recalling Houdon rather than the rhetoric of post-Napoleonic French sculpture. This modest but assured *métier* combines strangely with the bare and forthright tradition of woodworking he had experienced earlier. Romania is a heavily forested land, and wood was and is in evidence every-where for the construction and decoration of houses, churches, furniture, farm implements, carts, grave-markers. Often wood is employed in the frankest and simplest way, trimmed straight and forked branches being used

33 Romanian farm cart

as the unadorned components of the ubiquitous farm cart. The 'peasant carving' of Brancusi's childhood represents not simply a store of motifs from the primitive ready to be deployed in a more sophisticated milieu, but the experience of the direct and practical use of an essential material in an economically backward but culturally rich environment.[1]

In 1904 Brancusi arrived in Paris, undoubtedly drawn by Rodin's reputation. He worked from the model at the Beaux-Arts; he made many small heads and busts, including several for portrait commissions; after showing at the Salon d'Automne in 1906, where his work favourably impressed Rodin, he possibly worked for a time in the master's studio, until he was released by the commission for *The Prayer* from Romania.[2] The fruits of this first three years in Paris were modest enough, in terms of sculpture; but the period was of enormous importance in Brancusi's development, as a time in which he could measure himself against the standards and expectations Rodin had created for sculpture, both in his own work and in the work of those considered his heirs, among whom was evident an increasing dissatisfaction with Rodin's increasingly rhetorical articulation of surface, and his incapacity to make the actuality of each sculpture – its final form, size and material – a substantive and necessary part of the conception.[3] With the general collapse of academic opposition to Rodin in the 1880s the lack of a defined and determined structure for the newly-won independence of modelled volume had gone largely overlooked, although Rodin himself clearly sought out monumental commissions as a means of limiting and compressing the centrifugal tendencies in his work. However, with increasing public acclaim, commercial demand became the main determinant of the final form, and enlargements, reductions, transpositions into marble, together with great numbers of casts of the most popular pieces, all tended to obscure what was strong and original in Rodin's sculpture (as indeed they still do).

Maillol, Bourdelle, and most successfully Matisse, were variously attempting to reintroduce some sort of definition and structure, but still in terms of the treatment of the total figure, and of the tradition of public sculpture that Rodin had re-vitalized. But it needed the detachment of a sculptor brought up in an alien tradition to recognize that these components were the externals of Rodin's achievement; Brancusi had experience of a direct and objective handling of material, in his case, wood, and of a compact and enclosed convention, the portrait bust. He perceived that the core of Rodin's achievement resided in the relation with the material. The process of modelling clay, the realization of volume in soft, self-adhesive material, implies an additive mode, with no natural end-form or distinctive outer limit. The direction of Rodin's art, and of modelling itself, is outwards into the spectator's space. Rodin's sculpture reaches out for a response; from the modelling process springs its 'publicness'; the assumption of the public tradition was a consequence, not a motive, of his art.

Brancusi's opportunity was to isolate carving, as Rodin had isolated modelling, as the fundamental determinant of sculpture. Rodin had neglected or misused carving as outrageously as had his academic predecessors. Brancusi saw in carving the means to the definitive and unique final form for each sculpture. Carving had been exclusively the province of craftsmen, both in the studios of the leading academic sculptors of the day, and in the hundreds of small workshops where funerary sculpture was produced to order. The sheer quantity of this work should not necessarily lead us to despise or dismiss it, if only for the degree of skill and patience involved; moreover, the category of funerary sculpture represents, with the tradition of the portrait bust, another strain in the Western sculptural tradition opposite to that of the heroic public monument revived by Rodin – the private monument, witnessing the life or death of an individual, as remembered by his family or locality. The connection between the tradition of the individual monument and the revival of carving by Brancusi is evident. Again it was not Brancusi himself, but the painters Gauguin and Derain who first turned to direct carving in wood and stone: but it needed Brancusi, a sculptor for whom the carving tradition was still alive, to exploit and develop their discovery.

Whereas modelling in Rodin's hands, however intimate the subject-matter, had become public, aggressive, extravert and generalized, Brancusi realized carving as the opposite mode: private, individual, separate, concentrated and quiet. Carving is reductive from a given limit, but seeks to affirm

43

the given qualities of that limit. The spectator is visually and intellectually drawn in to the illusioned area between the potential of the block, the untouched wood or stone, and the actuality of the sculpture-object. Nonetheless, carving was not for Brancusi himself a mystique but a method, whose practicality and concreteness were its central virtues.

Brancusi's final student piece, the *Ecorché* in the pose of the classical Antinous, and all the surviving early work from Paris, can be cited to demonstrate that his sensibility was that of a carver even before he actually started to cut directly into stone. He clearly preferred to work within given limits, with a clear and simple division and articulation of forms, and a taut and crisp overall treatment of surface. The portrait bust provided a conventional format within which the human form could be curtailed without unnecessary drama, and it may be argued that the typical vertical organization of all Brancusi's later sculpture, with the precisely-defined sculpture-object placed on a simpler and more generalized pedestal, represents the persistence of the portrait bust convention.

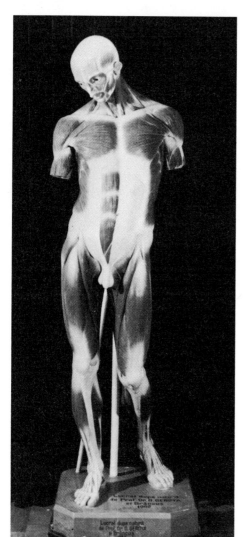

34 CONSTANTIN BRANCUSI *Ecorché*
1902

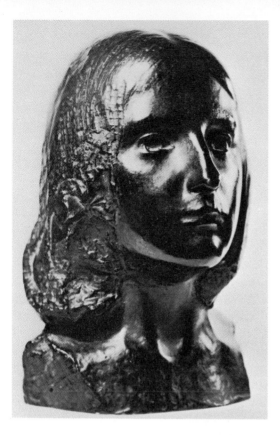

35 CONSTANTIN BRANCUSI *Pride*
1905

Brancusi continued to struggle with the extended total figure in the clay studies he worked on at the Beaux-Arts, but he did not cast or retain them. It was not until *The Prayer* (1907), when he discovered how to contain the figure within a rigorous geometric structure, that he managed to rid himself of this obsession. In *The Kiss*, which was his second direct stone-carving,[4] the 'natural' rectangle of the limestone block replaces the 30°–60°–90° triangular profile which had been imposed on the earlier modelled figure. *The Prayer* discharges Brancusi's immediate debt to Rodin; thereafter he can exploit Rodin's discovery of material as the fundamental determinant of form, without any obligation to rival his central theme, that of the complete human figure. In various other respects, also, Brancusi was to develop rather than subvert Rodin. Common titles – *The Kiss, A Muse, Danaid, The Prodigal Son, Adam, Eve* and so on – indicate a continuity of ambition; Brancusi's famous 'themes', progressive refinements of a given motif, represent a re-examination of the repertory of stock figures used by Rodin and earlier sculptors. The idea of the studio as the proper place to look at the sculpture, the acknowledgment of the sculptor as the creator of his own world, not the decorator of someone else's: all these were elements that Brancusi certainly inherited from Rodin.

Brancusi's first carvings were made in limestone, in 1907. The following year he began to work directly in marble. His first wood carving was not executed until 1913. Each material tended to produce a particular formal category of object – determined by the shape of the material in its raw state, and by its structural properties. Thus, after a few early and erratic attempts to carve *into* the stone (*Wisdom of the Earth*, 1907, *Double Caryatid*, 1908), the block is increasingly 'preserved' as the sculpture in itself, until, in the later versions of *The Kiss*, the image is indicated solely by lines incised in the surface of the coarse stone.

The typical form of the denser, more closely-packed marble, and the bronzes cast from marble, is the egg, the kernel at the centre of the block: the form is enlarged to include neck, shoulders, even hands, as in *Mlle Pogany*, *Princess X*, *A Muse*; extended and tapered, as in the *Birds*; flattened and balanced on edge, as in the *Fish*; but the conception remains constant in relation to the material.

Wood offered the greatest variety of possible end-forms for Brancusi: the square and round vertical column, the grain giving possibility of almost infinite extension; and the suggestion of articulated forms derived from the natural forking of the original timber.[5]

36 CONSTANTIN BRANCUSI
Mlle Pogany 1912

37 CONSTANTIN BRANCUSI *The Kiss* 1911(?)

38 CONSTANTIN BRANCUSI *Timidity* 1915

The first *Kiss* (1907) is not only the model for Brancusi's later treatment of stone; it is a symbolic sculpture, unique in the œuvre, signifying a clean break with the past. If *The Prayer* looks backward, *The Kiss* looks forward. Its form is that of a design conceived in the mind rather than arrived at by a continuous process of adjustment, as with almost all Brancusi's other themes. Once stated, the motif is merely clarified in subsequent versions. (*Timidity* of 1915 indicates a second, quite distinct, method of handling stone, while preserving the blockiness and stability of the *Kiss* motif.) Yet, in spite of its conceptual completeness and its apparent simplicity and predictability, *The Kiss* reveals, to a greater extent than *The Prayer*, an affectionate and naturalistic concern for human detail. The two bodies seem compressed together by some great force, rather than being the two halves of a symmetrically divided block; and the anatomical absurdity of the design, in identifying wrist and elbow at the turn of the block, is corrected by the beautifully observed distinction between the character of the male and female hands.[6]

47

39 CONSTANTIN BRANCUSI *Sleeping Muse* 1909–11

Brancusi's definitive form for marble was first arrived at with *The Sleeping Muse* of 1910: the portrait head removed from its neck and shoulders; the features in process of absorption into the continuous surface; the orientation of the form, its relation to gravity, starting to determine its internal proportions. For the first time, Brancusi cast from marble into bronze. Bronze becomes a carving material for Brancusi, something other than a means of making clay permanent. He worked on the bronzes, making each cast individually different, and from the marble *Prometheus* made his first highly polished bronze. The features have virtually disappeared; expression is generated by the diagonal axis of the head and the vestigial neck. Polishing is the last refinement of carving, the abrasion and removal of fractional quantities of material. The reflective surface must surpass in perfection the smooth and translucent marble; in the bronze, it becomes a container for the image of the spectator and the environment, shaped and modulated in the form of the object.

48

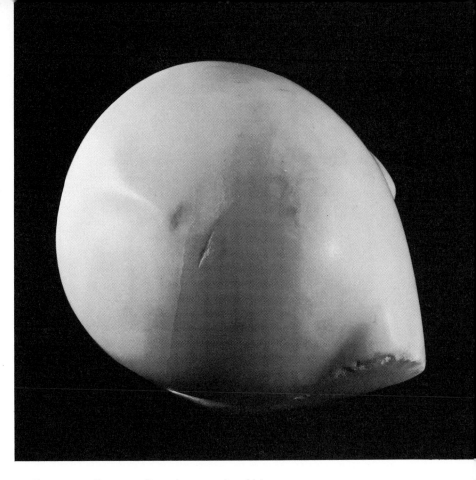

40 Constantin Brancusi *Prometheus* 1911 (marble)

41 Constantin Brancusi *Prometheus* 1911 (bronze)

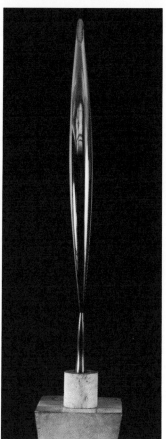

In 1911 Brancusi breaks out of the remaining constrictions of human subject-matter with the first bird, the *Maiastra*; though the form is still basically a head and neck, the handling of the marble has an enhanced definition which speaks of an increasing confidence with the material, and from the possibilities of invention attendant on the disappearance of the obsessive need to identify traces of the human image. Over the next fifteen years, Brancusi developed the bird theme with growing audacity in an inspired dialogue between marble and bronze. Ironically, marble, the material of academic perfection in the nineteenth century, was unable to sustain the structural demands Brancusi made in the progressively more ambitious and more attenuated versions of the *Bird in Space* from 1928 onwards.[7]

While marble and polished bronze became the vehicles of thematic compression and refinement, Brancusi's discovery of wood afforded a means of re-entry into articulated form, without following traditional modes of articulation derived from the human body. Almost certainly it was the stimulus of Cubism, with its emphasis on the breakdown of unitary forms, that prompted Brancusi to turn to wood, with its long grain and tensile

50

42 Constantin Brancusi *Măiastră*
1912

43 Constantin Brancusi *Bird in Space* 1941

44 Constantin Brancusi *The Prodigal Son* 1915

strength, in which the definition and separation of form could be achieved swiftly and decisively with the saw and axe.

This use of wood, at once so radical and so natural, was not preconceived, but arose out of a series of experiments, starting, as with his first use of marble, from a strongly naturalistic basis. Both the peasant carving of his native Romania, and African art, provided him with models for the clear and decisive handling of wood. Indeed, the universal interest in African art at the time must have been more of an embarrassment than a guide to Brancusi: where Picasso and Braque were free to borrow the formal simpli- fications of African carving and transfer them almost without modification into their own painting, such literal transposition was clearly impossible for Brancusi when he was working in the same medium. His first attempts to resolve this difficulty consisted in combining a European motif – walking child, caryatid – with stylized, 'primitive' handling of the parts of the body. Then, in *The Prodigal Son* (1915), the naturalistic overall organization is abandoned for an almost abstract and mechanical division of forms, appar- ently achieved largely by a number of saw cuts through a rectangular block (though the image remains that of a compressed caryatid).

It was not until *The Sorceress* (1916) that Brancusi found the ideal solution: an articulation into parts not imposed by style or decoration, or by an emphatic use of tools, but inherent in the material itself. That is to say, an already articulated, naturally forked piece of timber replaces the conventional block, and in effect becomes the motif of the sculpture. Although from time to time Brancusi made constructed wood sculptures – i.e. works combining separate, ready-shaped pieces of wood – he clearly found the lack of integrity in the work in progress disturbing, and preferred to feed back the possibility of an implied free relation of parts into monolithic carvings like the *White Negress* and *Leda*. From the discovery of *The Sorceress* derives a great series of individual and thematic sculptures: the *Torso of a Young Man*, *The Cock*, and *The Turtle*, all carved in the first instance from a naturally forked piece of wood. These sculptures are distinct from the rest of Brancusi's œuvre in that their compact internal structure implies through the use of sections the infinite penetration of space along every axis. They are tense and dramatic, but wholly without rhetoric. Their complexity refers them to body, rather than head, in terms of human physical equivalence – in both the late, large, *Cocks* and *The Turtle* Brancusi dispensed with the base, which plays the role of 'body' in presenting the majority of his 'head' objects. This final group, challenging as it does the simple architectural symmetry of the limestone pieces and the ideal refinement of form and finish of the bronze/ marble sculptures, remains for me Brancusi's major achievement (setting aside the Tîrgu Jiu group). It shows the artist daring to question the aesthetic which he had created out of the single-minded intensity of the early years: an aesthetic which, when relaxed, hovered close to the sweetly decorative.

45 Constantin Brancusi *The Sorceress* 1916

46 Constantin Brancusi *Adam and Eve* 1921

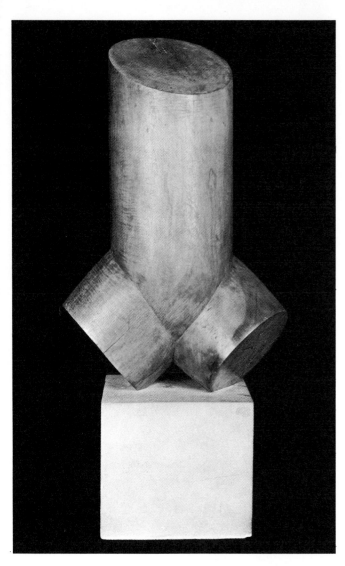

47 Constantin Brancusi *Torso of a Young Man* 1916

48 Constantin Brancusi *The Turtle* 1943

49 Constantin Brancusi *The Cock* 1924

Brancusi did not apply himself seriously to making bases until 1918, well into his most intense period of activity in woodcarving. One can see how ambitious pieces such as the *Caryatids* (1915), *Adam* (1917), *Chimera* (1918) and the first *Endless Column* (1918), which all started naturally from the ground, must have drawn Brancusi's attention both to the uneasiness of the earlier small sculptures' relation to the environment, and to a possible solution of this problem.

In contrast to the wood and stone sculptures, the bronze and marble pieces are relatively small, 'precious', in relation to other objects in general, and generally unstable, that is to say, balanced on a point, or touching curved volume to flat surface. As the objects left the protected environment of the studio, the control of the sculptor in presenting them, in determining their relationship with the spectator and other objects, could be preserved by the device of the carved base: it would present the object at the correct height, physically secure it from damage, maintain a precisely determined orientation, and mediate between the refinement of the object, its intense differentiation, and the undifferentiated nature of an alien environment. As the germinative theme of Brancusi's marble sculptures is the human head, conceived as a total object in detachment from the body, so the base can be seen as having to play the part of the shoulders and neck of the traditional portrait bust: all the expression is concentrated into the head, or object, which is the focus of our attention: but it is articulated towards us by a structure which echoes or enhances the object, without competing with it: which reinforces its unity and totality.

Neither the limestone nor the wood sculptures are at ease with the constructed base: the former because their four-square stability, their internal architecture, calls for a more solid relation with the earth, finally achieved in the *Gate of the Kiss*; the latter because their complexity and dynamism, their relative freedom and spontaneity, duplicate those very qualities with which Brancusi increasingly imbued the bases.

It has been said that Brancusi's bases have the same function as the painted frames of Seurat,[8] which form a gradation between the privileged reality of the painting and the habitual reality of the wall. But the base is far more crucial structurally to the sculpture than the frame is to painting. With or without the frame, the picture is suspended on the wall by supports which are taken for granted and usually invisible; whereas the base in sculpture is the support as well as the visual setting: it not only mediates between the object and the world, but, coming between the object and the ground, represents the world in terms of its gravitational pull in immediate contiguity to the object. The role of the base is at once physical, in terms of support; visual, in terms of presenting the object at proper level; and symbolic, in terms of the object's relation with the world. The bases are not works of art,

50 CONSTANTIN BRANCUSI
Fish 1926

but are as worth consideration as many works of art in view of the way they perform an exact ancillary function. Most of Brancusi's sculpture is modest in size, physically unobtrusive. Yet its presence is enormous even from a considerable distance, and where surrounded by the work of other artists. The Brancusi is marked off by its carved and constructed base as being not only different from other things in general, but as being different from all other sculpture, *a completely new order of object*. Brancusi evidently considered his studio as the ideal environment for his work as a group. The base plays the role of the studio as environment in relation to the individual work. Where the sculpture is polished, the base is rough; where the sculpture is tight and ordered, the base is free and playful; where the sculpture is concentrated, the base is expansive.

The base is only part of Brancusi's work, but it is an indication of his genius that he could apply so much skill and invention to an area that most artists would regard as mere presentation.

The base has another aspect. It carries the finish of the object one stage further – carving is taken beyond the most perfect surface, the highest polish, to the point where the action of the sculptor in making the object reaches and touches the action of the spectator in experiencing it. Rodin, the modeller, is the sculptor as *initiator*: his sculpture has the energy of beginning, the first touch; and the necessity of casting into bronze, copying into marble, means that the craftsman and executant intervene; the immediacy of the final sculpture, its closeness to the spectator, is an illusion dependent on the technical work of many hands. Brancusi took carving to be the reverse of this process: his is the last hand to touch the object; he is the sculptor as finisher.

Brancusi's proclaimed concern with the 'essential' in sculpture belies the apparent modesty of the work, and reveals an ambition to put himself beyond history and criticism. His sculpture, to say nothing of his life, has been treated by gullible admirers as though there were no active relation between the artist, his predecessors, contemporaries and successors; and Brancusi's encouragement of his own myth reinforces the impression of a perfectly sealed-off cycle of existence in which elements of the work and the life become virtually interchangeable. Attention to the rough edges of his biography, for example to his worldliness and professionalism, is not in itself enough to bring Brancusi back into history. We need a really detailed and serious exploration of the development of sculptural thinking in Paris in the early years of the century.[9] We need most of all to recognize that quality of groping, of imperfection, of dissatisfaction with the accessible and merely emblematic solution, that characterizes Brancusi's best work, and is only to be revealed by the persistence in the sculpture of our own time of the rich veins that Brancusi opened up.

3 Picasso:
Cubism and Construction

Nothing could present a more vivid contrast to Brancusi's hard-won liberation from Rodin, within the continuity of a *sculpture* tradition, than the audacity of Picasso's constructions in wood, cardboard, paper, string and other materials, of 1912–14; and it is a strange paradox that these most radical of works should be so modest, drab, even furtive in presence, in contrast for example to the enormous attack, vigour, and freshness that *Les Demoiselles d'Avignon* has even today. It is true that these constructions can be seen as the natural and inevitable development from Cubist collage; but the inevitability is that of history and hindsight. In the event, Braque faltered as he got to the point of three-dimensional collage, and Picasso dropped this line of activity completely after a couple of years, returning to it much later when the moment of urgency had passed, with more facility and more ambition, but less real success.

These constructions, thought of as sculpture or painting pure and simple, are objects beyond justification by any traditional precedent. As painting, all that remains of the frame, the picture rectangle, pictorial space itself, exists in the relationships of those parts of the structure which stand for depicted objects or parts of depicted objects; these are physical relationships, simultaneous with the illusioned ones, the actual joining and fixing of wood, string and nails. Painting gives way to physical making, and survives only to key or differentiate existing parts. The picture surface has been replaced by the frontal planes of real volumes, although the orientation of the whole is still pictorial – that is forward to the spectator, back to the wall – and the illusion of deeper volume, of implied perspective, of modelled, rounded surfaces, is still consequently present. When one considers the *Musical Instrument* of 1914, the problem of representation is no longer an issue. The internal ordering of the parts preponderates over the schematic references to reality, so that, although the point of departure may be necessary for the artist, it is no longer so for us. It no longer helps to be able to identify it as a guitar or mandolin; it has become a self-sufficient object.

As sculpture, these constructions are probably even more radical. Even if considered within the convention of relief, with modelled shallow volumes giving the illusion of a deep recession, they do things with material, process and subject-matter that had simply never existed as a possibility in sculpture before. The human figure, in whole or in part, in bronze, carved wood or stone, was even at that time, even for the most advanced artists, the main constituent of sculpture; and Picasso in this brief assault not only demonstrated that sculpture could do without these historic sanctions on material and subject-matter, but gave sculpture a potential freedom, the implications of which are still being worked out. It was due solely to Picasso, and in particular to the pieces under discussion, that it became possible to literally 'make' a piece of sculpture, for the first time in history – that is to say, to assemble it out of parts, as a craftsman would a table or a chair. It is difficult to exaggerate the importance of this discovery for sculpture, because it is so commonplace to us now, and because it has always existed as fundamental to invention in all the arts. 'You can't make a poem with ideas. . . . *You make it with words,*' as Mallarmé is notoriously supposed to have said to Degas;[1] poetry is the Greek *poiesis,* 'making'; the idea of the art-work constructed of parts, related in a harmonious whole, is as old as the discussion of art itself. Yet, until Picasso, the possibility of the free arrangement of parts to create an expressive whole had been precluded, in sculpture, by the insistence on a restricted range of subject-matter, and on certain prescribed and durable materials, with their concomitant processes and formal restrictions.

Both Brancusi and Matisse were working at the same period within these accepted limits. Though both profoundly affected by Cubism, they still worked from within the same conventions that Picasso had burst open. And although Picasso lost interest or nerve in this direction after 1915, and left it to others to exploit his strike until he returned to construction in the late 1920s, the significance of these pieces should not be underrated. The barrier, after all, was a mental, not a physical one; still-life was a time-honoured subject for painting; there was nothing physically new about his materials or their mode of assembly. It needed his inspired opportunism to cross the two factors, to produce a new strain that was to transform sculpture.

It is true that the implications of Cubist innovations in painting and collage were already being explored by forward-looking sculptors in Paris. Boccioni, Archipenko and Laurens, among others, were using wood, metal, cardboard, glass, as sculpture material; and their handling of these materials is far more sophisticated and assured than that of Picasso. Equally, Boccioni's famous *Development of a Bottle in Space* (1912) marks a breakthrough in the *subject-matter* of sculpture contemporary with Picasso's first constructions.[2] Whatever the relationship in time, the authority of Picasso's constructions lies partly in their consistency in the sequence of Cubism, and partly in their directness of response to the materials, their straightforward crudity of construction unalloyed by preconceptions of style or taste.

52 Pablo Picasso *Houses on a Hill, Horta* 1909

Clearly, Cubism triggered off a general outburst of activity in sculpture that in many ways outstripped the ambition and intentions of the authors of Cubism. Nevertheless, many of these manifestations were more declamatory than substantial; only Raymond Duchamp-Villon and Jacques Lipchitz were to make Cubist sculpture of permanent quality, and their approach to materials and subject-matter was conventional.[3] In terms of its early impact the lesson of Cubism for sculpture was in the separation, clarification, and rationalization of form; the acceptance of construction into the mainstream of the sculpture tradition had to wait until Picasso made his second incursion into the field, this time using iron and the assistance of Julio González.

But because first Braque, then Picasso, withdrew when Cubist collage threatened to detach itself completely from the picture surface, and proceeded to put the discoveries of the previous few years into the making of oil paintings, the history of Cubism has been written from the viewpoint of the restructuring of pictorial space. The effect of Cubism on painting was total, immediate and spectacular, but it was an effect on *style*. The results in sculpture were far more profound and lasting: from the perspective of today, the

53 PAUL CÉZANNE *Rocky Landscape, Aix* 1885

development of Cubism from its beginning in 1907, long before it actually moved into 3 dimensions, looks ineluctably part of the history of modern sculpture.

Les Demoiselles d'Avignon is usually taken to be the first Cubist painting; and from 1907 until 1909 the subject-matter of Picasso's and Braque's paintings was conventional enough, consisting of nude figures, singly or in groups, landscape, and still-life. Each type of subject called for a certain kind of pictorial structure, the grouping or dispersion of areas of interest, the breakdown of recognizable subject into planes and illusioned volumes. In this first stage of Cubism, landscape provided an ideal pretext for making what was virtually an abstract structure.

If one compares Picasso's *Houses on a Hill*, painted at Horta in 1909, with a comparable painting by Cézanne, the *Rocky Landscape, Aix* (1885), one notes immediately that the Picasso painting is far more sculptural in effect, besides being, obviously, far more generalized and abstract. Although the illusioned space in the Cézanne is much deeper, the colour, the presence of individually-defined brushmarks, and the even dispersion of interest, make one strongly aware of the picture as a painted surface. By contrast, the interest is strongly in the centre of the Picasso picture, although each unit is lit separately, as opposed to the natural lighting from one direction in the Cézanne; this contributes to the intensity of the sculptural illusion. The depth of the Cézanne picture is visual; in the Picasso depth is almost tactile – one explores it with the hand as much as with the eye.

By 1910 Braque and Picasso had begun to break into the contours of depicted shapes and the surrounding space to create an overall pattern of planes, in the manner that came to be known as Analytical Cubism. The consequent even distribution of emphasis over the picture rectangle might seem a move in the direction of the pictorial and away from the sculptural illusion of separately depicted volumes (as in the Horta landscape). However, this effect is counteracted by the subject-matter of the pictures of the Analytical period: these are mostly half-length portraits or still-lifes, providing a strong central cluster of interest, with a definite orientation to gravity – that is to say, the implied structure is built on the bottom margin of the picture

54 GEORGES BRAQUE *Still-life with Fish c.* 1909–11

55 PABLO PICASSO *Female
Nude, Cadaqués* 1910

rectangle, which works like a base, as in Braque's *Still-life with Fish* of 1911.
In the *Female Nude* of 1910 Picasso dispenses with the faceting of the background completely, and the figure reads so strongly as an illusioned construction that I imagine it would not be too difficult to make physically with sheet
steel or plywood (as Gabo was virtually to do in his constructed steel *Head* of
1916).

The commonplace subject-matter of Cubist still-life – glasses, dishes,
guitars, violins, pipes and so forth – became for contemporaries as much a
hallmark of Cubist painting as the new pictorial structure itself. However,
the intention was not aggressive; it was to neutralize the importance of the
subject, to turn it into *object*, by taking its existence for granted. In terms of
subject, as well as handling, the Analytical Cubist still-life was virtually
abstract. The conventional elements of still-life present a ready-made linear
vocabulary: the violin, for example, provides a variety of curves – the
profile of the sound-box, the f's of the sound-holes, the scroll at the top –

contrasting with the parallel or converging straight lines of the strings. The separation of these linear elements was the prelude to their translation later into physical, constructional terms.

Still-life as a genre implies the preliminary construction of the subject by the painter, before he starts work on the canvas. The still-life is an artificial, 'made' thing; the Cubists first dispensed with the need to work from reality and from there it was a short step to presenting the constructed still-life as an art object itself, without the need to filter it through the conventions of pictorial representation.

Until the introduction of collage, the sculptural in Cubism remained in the realm of illusion. When Braque and Picasso actually started to cut out and paste up pieces of textured paper, newspaper and so on, they moved into the area of physical making. A tool – knife or scissors – was introduced into the process, and although the collage still reads by reference and illusion, cutting and glueing stand for a mode that is far more concrete than that implied by the use of brush and pencil. In fact, both Braque and Picasso start to use the drawn line in conjunction with collage elements in a far more actual, concrete way, as though they were using a saw, or wire, rather than charcoal. More-

56 PABLO PICASSO *Glass, Bottle and Guitar* 1912

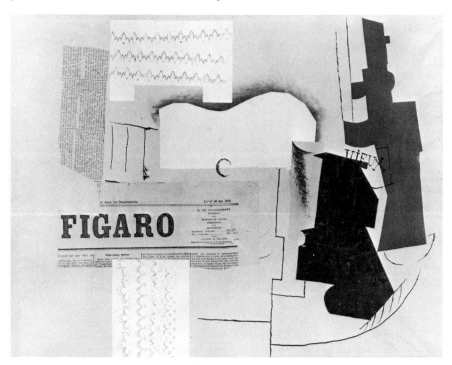

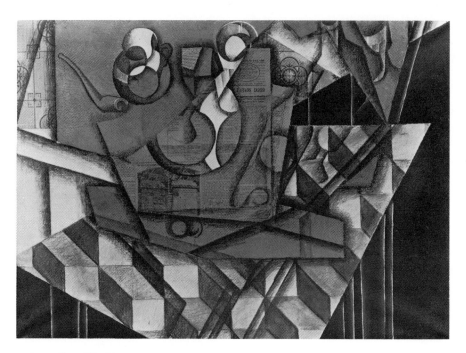

57 JUAN GRIS *The Teacups* 1914

over, the central coherence of the elements as a group that is physically bonded and interwoven, noticeable in the Analytical period, now becomes dominant: the central nucleus becomes an object for which the surrounding rectangle no longer offers support. (The characteristic oval frame of the Cubist painters also confirms the need to tie the elements of the painting into a central structure, rather than depend on the character of the rectangle to generate an internal structure proper to itself.) It is instructive to compare the construction of, say, Picasso's *Glass, Bottle and Guitar* of 1912 with Juan Gris' collage *The Teacups* of 1914. In the latter collage the individual elements – cups, glasses, plates, pipe and so on – are far more 'sculpturally' realized than in the Picasso, but nonetheless they are embedded in a composition derived from a division of the picture rectangle into areas each of which is then given a specific character, of flatness, of modelling, of implied depth or projection; the power of the picture operates on our awareness of the tension between the whole as a flat rectangle and the parts as areas with conflicting indications of volume and space. From 1915, Picasso took up this option of working against the confines of the rectangle, often making up for a certain slackness of composition by variety of strong colour and texture and by the witty use of sign references to the subject.

67

In 1912 both Braque and Picasso were making constructions in paper, most of which (and all of Braque's) have disappeared; Braque went no further in this direction, but Picasso started to employ more durable materials – cardboard, string, wood and thin sheet steel. Picasso was enormously responsive to the most immediately available characteristics of a material; for this reason the wooden constructions strike me as being by far the strongest of the group. In the metal pieces the crudity of the folding disturbs, whereas the crudity of the carpentry in the wooden pieces does not. The continuous metal sheet is too reminiscent of the picture plane, and is not sufficiently differentiated into separate parts by the making process; and so Picasso has to mark them off by garish colour or texture. Similarly, the generally overrated *Glass of Absinth* retains the flabbiness of the wax from which it was originally modelled, in contrast to the wooden structures of the same year, 1914, which

58 PABLO PICASSO *Glass and Dice* 1914

59 PABLO PICASSO *Guitar* 1914

60 PABLO PICASSO *Glass, Pipe and Playing-card* 1914

are admittedly more pictorial, but are fundamentally more daring and original. The cutting, shaping and fixing of the elements of wood and other materials, and the persistence of given reality elements – dice, glass, guitar, etc. – provide a natural extension to the kind of process that emerged from collage. Sawing and fixing provided a closer analogy to the process of conceptual reconstruction of reality involved in drawing than folding could provide. Most importantly, the process involves the bonding of separate parts each of which the artist endows with individual character. The wood pieces also score in that the material has a degree of thickness, of volume, whereas the paper and metal constructions have only plane. The wood works simultaneously as structure, as plane (representing fragments of the dis-membered picture plane), and as volume, both illusioned (that is to say representing deeper volume) and real, as where the rectangular element at the bottom of *The Musical Instrument* thrusts straight out at the spectator. The complexity and density of space and reference that has been noted in Picasso's collages proper is intensified in these constructions.

The finest of this group of pieces is the *Still-life with Fringe* of 1914, now in the Tate Gallery. In this object, painting, collage and sculpture achieve a momentary and miraculous equilibrium. Unlike the *Musical Instrument*, which is a transformation of an existing object, playing with a known gestalt, the *Still-life with Fringe* is a wholly new object, a compound image of several separate and still recognizable things. The subject is familiar to painting, and all the immediately visible surfaces are painted, except for the fringe; but the powerful and irregular profile, its quality as cohesive nucleus, the build-up of layers of uniform thickness and varied texture, indicate collage; then the deliberately unpainted end-grain of the planks against the wall, and the raw wood in the gouged holes in the bread; the unconcealed nail-heads; the projecting sections of the crudely 'analysed' glass, the use of the tipped shelf or table top to thrust bread, knife and fringe into a 'real' space, free of the wall – these details of material and construction declare it to be sculpture. Around the projecting ellipse of the shelf – the element of the object that comes closest to the spectator – there dangles the fringe, the motif and colour of which recall the heavily decorated gold frames enclosing Old Master paintings. The full dimensionality of the slices of bread and salami and of the knife, their verifiable location on the shelf enclosed by this illusioned frame, is paradoxically communicated as *less* tangible than the flattened, more abstract elements lying against the wall, with their bold overall contour and strong tonal contrast – the real cast shadows under the projecting sections of the glass, the dark wood-*grained* strip of dado, enlivened by the carved motif *painted* in effortless trompe-l'oeil. Actual if shallow carving invokes the transparent modulations of base, stem, and fluted side of the glass; the fluting is echoed in the knife-handle, in expectation the most

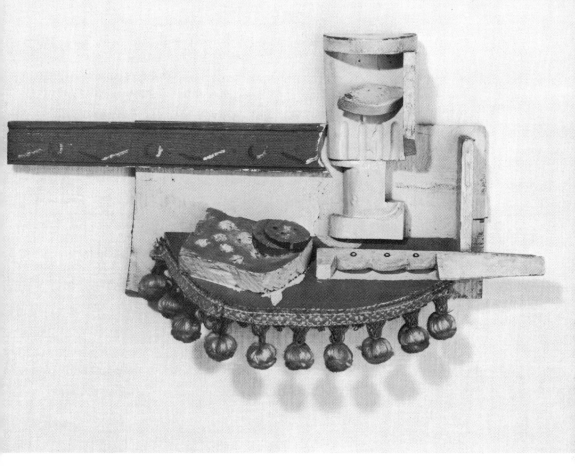

61 PABLO PICASSO *Still-life with Fringe* 1914

graspable volume of the ensemble, which is removed from use to decoration by the emphasis of the carved repeat design; while the blade moves toward graspability, becoming an exactly carved prism. And so on. One could meditate endlessly on the relations and illusions contained in this apparently most simple, clear and innocent of objects. This is Picasso at his very best, demonstrating the sensuous yet decisive manipulation of images, materials and space; a perfect balance of means and ends, of precise calculation and inspired improvisation: art conceals art with unrivalled tact and resource.

Apart from their richness and power as individual pieces, all these wooden constructions demonstrate the object-nature of modern sculpture. They take objects, still-life, as their subject-matter; they are constructed of the same material and in the same way as made objects in the world; and they have a completeness, an object-quality in themselves, an autonomy of structure and internal relations, that gives them an independence of any model in reality.

71

By comparison, the sculptures of Picasso's second period of construction (1929–31), made in collaboration with Julio González, have received far more attention, and were more immediately influential. Such sculptures as the *Woman in the Garden* of 1929, the *Construction in Wire* of 1930, the *Figure* of 1930–32, and the *Woman's Head* of 1931, are more obviously ambitious, more memorable as images, than the Cubist constructions, and are historically significant by virtue of the reintroduction of welded iron as a medium of equal seriousness and permanence to the traditional sculpture materials. Yet, expressive though these pieces are, they lack the economy, the compactness, the balance between means and ends, of the earlier pieces. They lack that character of internal self-sufficiency, as distinct from immediate effect, that becomes increasingly rare in Picasso's painting and sculpture (though it long persists in the graphic work, suggesting that it was ultimately in drawing, in line, that his genius lay). Compared to the *Construction in Wire*, for example, the drawings for *Le Chef d'œuvre inconnu* have a richness and variety, both of surface design and of spatial implication, that cannot be found in the sculpture.

The source of the unease created by the metal constructions seems to lie in two factors: Picasso's use of the human image, and his relation with his materials. By comparison with Matisse, for whom the figure in sculpture was

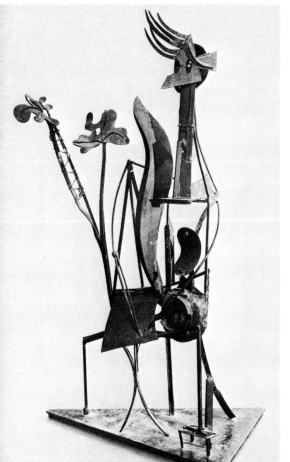

62 PABLO PICASSO *Woman in Garden* 1929–30

63 PABLO PICASSO *Construction in Wire* 1930

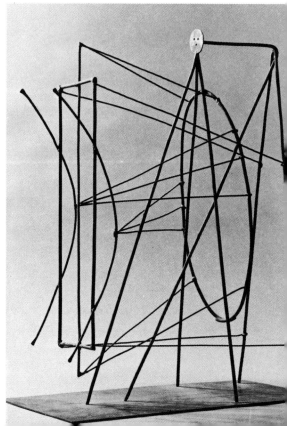

a point of departure, a schema upon which he could elaborate with virtually abstract freedom, the figure in Picasso's sculpture tends to become the point of arrival; the most abstract and diverse assemblages of parts are taken to the point at which they are resolved not through internal formal coherence but through the arbitrary imposition of human 'signs'. As for material, it is possible to perceive in the constructions of 1929–31 a gap between intention and execution, a lack of directness and technical resource, that is apparent neither in Picasso's Cubist constructions nor in the metal constructions that González was to execute on his own. The relation between Picasso and González apparently has much in common with that which earlier existed between Picasso and Braque: in both cases the volatile and impatient Picasso seems to have needed a slower, more timid, but more patient and technically more resourceful collaborator.

Whatever the conditions under which they originated, several of González's constructions of the 1930s are superior to the iron sculptures of Picasso, both in the inventive use of material and in the creation of symbolic, constructed equivalents for the human figure. What they lack in presence they more than make up for in the use of iron as a material equal in potential to bronze, wood and stone: the material proper to construction, as a mental and physical process.

64 PABLO PICASSO *Figure* 1930–32

65 PABLO PICASSO *Woman's Head* 1931

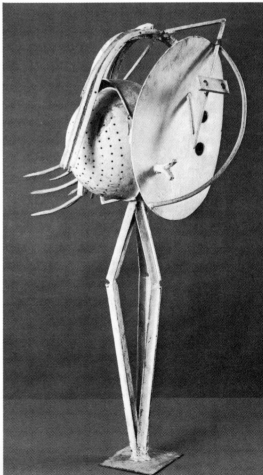

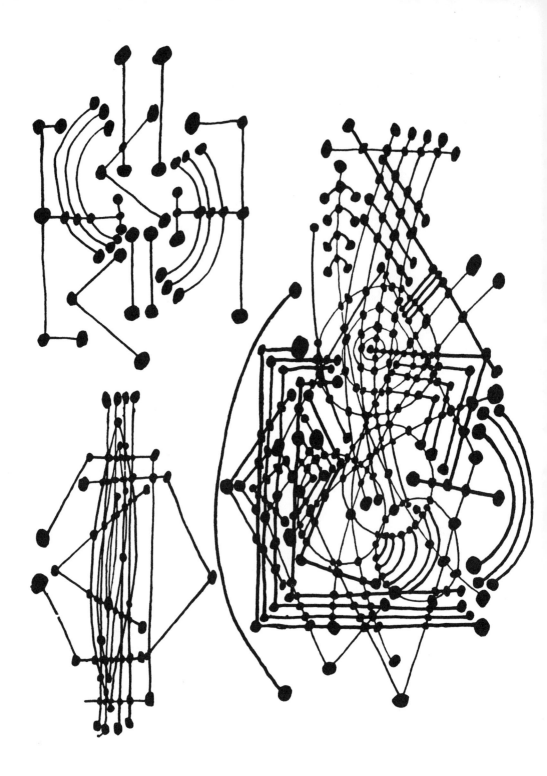

66 PABLO PICASSO *Drawing for 'Le Chef d'œuvre inconnu'* 1924

4 González

Julio González was born in Barcelona in 1876, the son and grandson of metal workers and jewellers. With his elder brother Joan, he was apprenticed in the family craft: together also they studied painting at the Escuela de Bellas Artes and frequented the avant-garde milieu of Barcelona in the 1890s, where they met the young Picasso. When the entire González family moved to Paris in 1900, Julio renewed this acquaintance. He was making his living, and had gained some reputation, as a craftsman in metal, but at this period of his life his aspiration as an artist centred on painting, in which his talent was no more than ordinary. González seems to have been pulled not only between the restrictions of his trade and the spiritual freedom enjoyed by the Bohemian circle around Picasso, but between the physical satisfaction to be gained from his craft, where his talent was real, and the emotional refuge provided by painting. These factors together help to explain the aestheticism and sentimentality of his work as a painter. The crisis was precipitated by the death of Joan in 1908: his elder brother had clearly given his own life a sense of purpose which González was unable to maintain alone. He withdrew from the avant-garde, and for the next eighteen years appears to have done little work with which he was satisfied. Of his artist friends he continued to see only Picasso and, probably, Brancusi.

He thus missed the development of Cubism entirely: but these two friendships were to prove of great importance when he eventually discovered himself in the late 1920s. For Picasso and Brancusi were the artists most notably responsible for the revolution in sculpture which occurred between 1909 and 1915. Brancusi applied the simplicity and rationality of craft procedures to the traditional materials of sculpture, thus in effect creating a new order of physical objects; while Picasso's Cubist constructions in 1912–15 demonstrated that sculpture could take its subject, structure, and material from the world of things. The way was prepared for González, unique among modern artists as a trained and practising maker of things.

It is Picasso who is generally credited with specifically introducing González to the possibilities of constructed metal sculpture by asking for his technical assistance in welding the celebrated series of metal sculptures of

1929–31. But González had already returned to creative activity with the sheet iron sculptures of 1926 onwards. While Picasso's liberated conception of what could be done in metal was crucial to González's development, it is quite possible that it was González's own recent work that had initially suggested the use of iron to Picasso. In any event, the active contact with Picasso both stimulated González and gave him the confidence he so urgently needed: the reassurance that the historic distinction between 'art' and 'craft' in sculpture which had come near to destroying him as an artist had now lost its meaning – that what had seemed a sign of inferiority now conferred a remarkable advantage.

González was a radical through circumstance rather than deliberate intent. By comparison with the other great masters of modern sculpture he seems to have been almost without ambition. His diffidence and modesty, his lack of confidence in the nature of his own gift, make him in retrospect a sympathetic figure; but one should remember that this lack of ambition cost him dear in practical terms: throughout his most productive period he barely scraped a living from sales. Iron was the favoured material not only for the qualities he was singularly well placed to exploit, but because it cost almost nothing from scrap. Still the victim of circumstance even when he had found his way in art, the pressure of poverty forced him to extract every possibility of expression from the material in a minor mode: to preclude for the most part the conscious making of monuments or masterpieces.

'Drawing in space' is the conventional summary of González's contribution to modern sculpture; and usually connotes the assembly in three dimensions of linear elements, as for example in the *Large Maternity* and the *Woman Combing her Hair*: the transposition of *line* drawing into sculpture. In this particular area the obvious precursor is Picasso, notably in the *Construction in Wire* of 1930. What is peculiar to González, and the index of his unique position in modern sculpture, is the *identification of drawing with making*. The seed of Picasso's original Cubist constructions in wood bore fruit in steel in the hands of González: not only the assembly part by part, but the previous and separate shaping of parts – bar forged, drawn or bent, sheet rolled, cut or folded, volumes made by the enclosure of the void: the components thus made, joined at points or edges, and situated in relation to gravity in ways inaccessible to the traditional materials of sculpture. The action of the sculptor's tools *becomes* the form of the end material: the tensile potential of steel 'as it comes' – i.e. in varieties of bar or sheet – is turned, in the sculptor's hands, to sheer invention.[1]

The entwined factors of poverty and lack of ambition make González essentially an explorer, a beginner: the provider of a multitude of clues and leads for others. In this he resembles Paul Klee, though Klee's confidence and sophistication reflect the incomparably greater resources of the painting

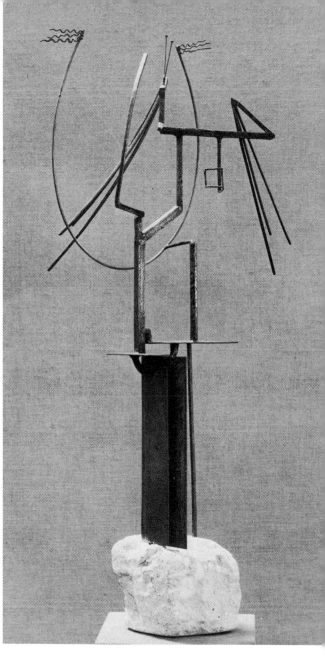

67 Julio González *Large Maternity* 1930–33

68 Julio González *Woman Combing her Hair* 1933–36

69 JULIO GONZÁLEZ *Small Head with a Triangle* 1934–36

70 JULIO GONZÁLEZ *Gothic Man* 1935

tradition. Like Klee, González is a miniaturist: his power lies in compression. Those works that seem to me his most satisfying and original are very small indeed – the group of heads originally executed in silver in the early 1930s. There is a clarity, an order and an invention about these sculptures that wholly subverts their physical size. In general, the larger González sculptures become, the more fussy and cluttered they tend to be, especially where different orders of component (i.e. linear, flat, solid) are in combination.

González also recalls Klee in the nature of his expression: a rational, even playful structure overlying a violent and tormented Expressionism. In González, it is a good deal nearer the surface than it is in Klee; and especially in the later 1930s it breaks through in such gruesome pieces as *Hand with Spikes*. Throughout the last twelve years of González's life there also recur the almost naturalistic heads, masks and figures of the *Montserrat* and *Crying Montserrat* series. These are not rhetorical: they rather reflect González's lack of confidence in the ability of his abstract and schematic mode to sustain the direct expression of powerful feeling. If we compare this naturalistic manner with the authority and vigour of, for example, the *Gothic Man*, we can see how mistaken González was in his estimation of the expressive power of his abstract style.

78

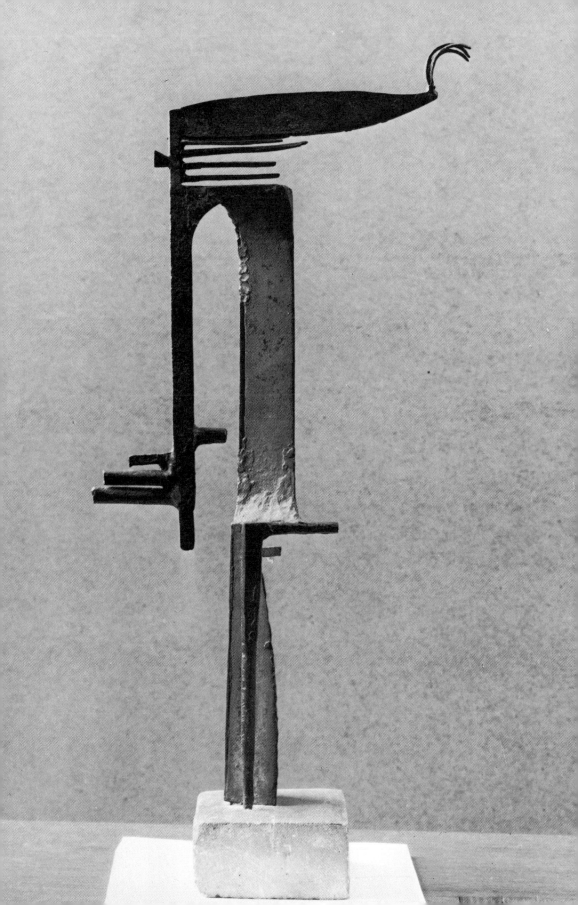

71 Julio González *Tunnel Head*
1933–35

A number of heads originally carved in stone, together with the early repoussé masks in copper and bronze, confirm that what was central to González's art was his conception of sculpture as modulated surface. The stone carvings reveal the failings of this approach when applied to an inappropriate material; but a marvellous series of constructions in sheet steel shows the range and control of González's most personal mode. The *Woman with Amphora* (recalling a later treatment by Matisse of the same theme) is a simply contoured cut-out in $\frac{3}{16}$ inch (5 mm) steel, daringly flat, formed only by the action of the saw through metal. In the *Mask of an Adolescent*, in thinner steel, the features are drawn with a maximum of economy by cutting and folding back from the plane. If one considers the curled edges and nuances of hammered shape in the *Foot*, the more complex cutting and folding (though still in the single plane) of the *Head*, the interlocking positive and negative of the *Mask, Light and Shade*, the beautifully subtle construction of angled and displaced, curved, bent and flat surfaces in *Head in Thought*, the creation of total darkness within a continuous surface by the almost complete sealing-off of the void within the *Tunnel Head*, one begins to get an idea of the expressive range González created with the simple articulation of surface by the separate action of tools. Conventional drawing, in the sense of contouring, is counterpointed by drawing as folding, rolling and fixing.

Unfortunately, the simple rationality of most of the sheet steel pieces is obscured by a kind of rustic, 'hand-made' insistence on texture. Here

González was presumably looking for an 'expressive' surface equivalent to the expressive imagery just mentioned; and also attempting to give iron the richness and density commonly associated with bronze.

It is in the working, and often the over-working, of parts that González's own metal contructions are distinct from those on which he collaborated with Picasso, and from the sculpture of his major successor, David Smith.[2] Picasso's metal constructions are unified by reference to the human image, and the parts left unmodulated save as they contribute to this effect; and Smith was to discover an abstract strength and variety in the given forms both of machine parts and steel from stock. By contrast González is very much the smith, working on each part before and after assembly; seeking and making parts for their affinity rather than their contrast; breaking down their separateness in the interests of an expressive unity. Both the strong sign references to elements of the figure and the characteristic forms of found parts, which are Picasso's stock in trade, are to be found in González, but one has to look hard for them. His own signs, notably that for hair, are far more generalized and ambiguous than Picasso's, acting more as relief or detail than specific reference, and arriving naturally by extension of the making process, the use of a particular tool. One can find unmodified elements of steel 'as it comes', as in the strips of T-section in *The Three Folds*, and the nails in the *Cactus-Men*. But the cylinders, cones and hemispheres that form the basis for many of González's sculptures are all consciously and wilfully crafted often to the point of concealing their fundamental geometry.

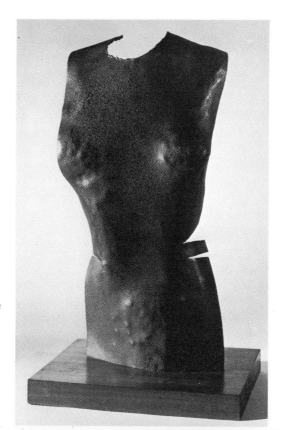

72 JULIO GONZÁLEZ *Bust of a Woman* c. 1935–36

73 JULIO GONZÁLEZ *Large Standing Figure c.* 1934

It is often assumed that González belongs to the European naturalistic and volumetric tradition in sculpture, which he and Picasso are held to have extended, not literally, but with sign and schema. That is to say, the conception is considered to be three-dimensional and figurative, even if the execution is linear and abstracted. This view seems to me to misconceive the nature of the original contribution of both González and Smith. The flatness of conception, the frontality and sign quality of Smith's sculpture, is anticipated in many of González's sculptures, though admittedly in the more ambitious pieces there is sufficient 3-dimensionality of articulation – for example the imaged (and classical) twist of the 'hips' in the *Large Standing Figure* – for the sculpture to remain legible 'in the round' rather than function simply and unequivocally as silhouette. The fundamental distinction between González and Smith is one of confidence and ambition: the physical and formal differences flow from this. González's sculpture is modest, made by

82

74 DAVID SMITH *25 Planes* 1958

and for the hand, and in feeling deeply pessimistic. Smith's work, certainly from 1950, is extravert, optimistic and positive; relating to the body rather than the hand, large in feeling as well as physical presence.

The originality and variety of González's work is largely obscured at the present time by the way in which the most accessible and superficial aspects of his style were absorbed by the great wave of textured and expressive sculpture, both constructed and modelled, figurative and abstract, that dominated taste in the post-war period. At a time when the idea of construction was revived to give life to a dying tradition of modelling, when form was sacrificed to texture and autonomy of structure to a cheap and melodramatic imagery, those elements of González's sculpture that simply and actively extend the fundamental and original contribution of Brancusi and Picasso were forgotten, except in so far as they reappeared in the work of David Smith.

75 David Smith *Sentinel III* 1957

5   The Sculpture of Matisse

Of the artists whose work is discussed in this book, Matisse's performance as a sculptor is, on first acquaintance, by far the least impressive. He made relatively few sculptures. They are almost all small; in terms of their material, their subject-matter, their ambience, they are wholly traditional; and yet, the more I look at Matisse's sculptures, the more I have come to realize how profoundly original they are. Matisse's acceptance of a traditional framework for his sculpture, partly through deliberate aesthetic inclination, partly through a sense of his own technical limitations, gives his work a peculiar freedom that is not to be found in any of his contemporaries.

Matisse has been described as a painter-sculptor, in the line of Daumier, Degas and Renoir,[1] and in many aspects this is true. His ambition was always in painting, and in painting he was to create his conscious masterpieces. In distinction to Picasso, whom one may fairly regard as a sculptor *manqué*, Matisse had to make a great effort to get used to the idea of working three-dimensionally. Many of Picasso's paintings, especially those from the Cubist period, as we have seen, have the character of depicted sculptural structures. Conversely, Matisse's sculpture, though it is never painterly in handling (in fact is far more intensely felt as *volume* than anything of Picasso's), nonetheless has the aesthetic character, the internality, the self-referential quality, of painting. Matisse has no monumental prejudice; none of the anxiety about the status of the work as an object, its relation to reality and the spectator, that has been one of the characteristic obsessions of sculpture since Rodin. It is this confidence in the sculpture-object as an architecture, as a harmonious relationship of parts to whole, that enabled Matisse to bypass the temptation of the arresting image that ensnared Picasso after his Cubist constructions. In Matisse's sculpture, as not always in his painting, there is *no desire to impress*. However modest and undemonstrative, almost all his sculpture radiates calm assurance in the total necessity of its existence.

Matisse himself was explicit about the role that sculpture played in his art. He says: 'I took up sculpture because what interested me in painting was a clarification of my ideas. I changed my method and worked in clay in order to have a rest from painting, where I had done all I could for the time being.

That is to say, it was done for the purposes of organization, to put order into my feelings and find a style to suit me. When I found it in sculpture, it helped me in my painting. It was always in view of a complete possession of my mind, a sort of hierarchy of all my sensations, that I kept working in the hope of finding an ultimate mastery.'[2]

Seen on its own, the sculptural œuvre presents an image so fragmented and discontinuous that neither a straightforward internal chronological treatment nor a division into various conventional sculpture categories – heads, figures, reliefs etc.– will pull the work together into a comprehensible sum or sequence. It is only when the spasmodic bursts of his activity in sculpture are seen in relation to the great span of his development in painting – which after all was itself by no means systematic or even consistent – that the work starts to come together. Only *The Back* relief series, of all the sculptures, have the look of conscious masterpieces, of public art. The sculpture is far more private than the painting, and fulfilled private needs which he was unable to satisfy in painting. Both the time he could spend on a sculpture without the danger of overworking, and the immediate and often violent involvement with clay, matter itself rather than its image, steadied him and, as he said, enabled him to put order into his feelings.

I have described the pervasiveness of Rodin's influence on sculpture at the turn of the century. The magnitude of Rodin's achievement in regaining for sculpture, for the first time since the Renaissance, its proper status as an independent art, largely inhibited, until about 1900, any serious and original exploitation of the territory he had opened up. But after 1900 a generation of artists was emerging in Paris who no longer identified Rodinesque modelling with sculptural expression: who were looking for a style in sculpture that would be ordered, economic, compact, undramatic, simple, related to modern life and to the increasing concreteness of painting. These aspirations were to be realized in the art of Brancusi and the Cubists. Compared to these sculptors, in the use of materials, in subject-matter and presence – the sculpture as object – Matisse in his own sculpture seems at first glance to have remained well within Rodin's field. Frequently one finds the description 'Rodinesque' applied to this or that piece of Matisse's sculpture; but the similarities are trivial compared with the differences. In fact, those sculptors who initially reacted strongly against Rodin, for example Lipchitz, in the long run owed him a much greater debt than did Matisse.

The correspondences that do exist between Rodin and Matisse derive from that strange split in Matisse's artistic personality: his need for precedent, his respect for tradition, in contrast to his love of risk in art; his slow and modest beginnings, in contrast to his capacious ambition and egotism. He had already been painting for ten years when he turned his hand to sculpture. In painting there were a multiplicity of models on whom he could base his developing

86

vision. In sculpture there was only one – Rodin. Though he had not found himself in painting when he came to sculpture, he had nonetheless gained from his experience a clear and mature idea of what he expected to find. 'I had already imagined on my own', he was to say later, 'a work of general architecture, replacing explicit details by a living and suggestive synthesis.'[3] Given Matisse's temperament and training one can see that he had no alternative but to work *through* Rodin, in terms both of material and the figure as subject.

But from the start Matisse's aims in sculpture were antithetic to Rodin's: Matisse was interested in the whole, not the part: in stability, balance, harmony, as against the illusion of movement, unbalance, the overly dramatic. Even the apparently common elements – the use of clay and the figure itself – turn out to be delusive. Rodin used clay with the intensity of working flesh itself. Matisse used clay like paint, quite naively and directly; clay was to him simply plastic volume material. He had no knowledge of, or interest in, the physical means as such. Rodin would add to or subtract from his sculptures; he was consciously and artfully *modelling*, in perfect control of his material. Matisse used clay that was too hard, and too soft: he carved and he modelled it; there is no style and little consistency in his handling. And yet, by virtue of this refusal or incapacity to respond to the conventional characteristics of his material and its craft employment, his sculpture retains a directness that is to do with the innocent experience of volume alone, without the intrusion of any knowledge or preconception. Similarly with the figure: whatever liberties Rodin may take with it, we are always conscious of anatomy, the tension and performance of bone and muscle; our knowledge of our own anatomy helps us to identify ambiguous and unspecified groups of masses, members and fragments. But with Matisse the figure is the given total: proportions and distortion within that whole are developed not in terms of a physical empathy with the spectator, of muscular expression, but in terms solely of an aesthetic ordering, a relation of parts. Compared, for example, with his friend Maillol who, however architectural his work appeared, remained tied to anatomic equivalence,[4] Matisse's sculpture from 1901 to 1907 was truly radical: indeed at this period and in this respect Matisse's sculpture was in fact, if not in impact, ahead of all his contemporaries in Paris.

Up until 1900 most of Matisse's paintings had been landscapes, interiors and still-lifes, apart from academic figure work. He was trying out a succession of styles and influences in painting, without having found an area large enough to contain his growing ambition. As a commentary on his own generalized account of why he took up sculpture, one notes that Matisse wanted to incorporate the figure into his art, and sculpture was the most direct way to approach the figure: he needed the continuity, the prolonga-

76 Henri Matisse *The Jaguar, after Barye* 1901

tion of work, in his first two main sculpture projects, *The Jaguar*, after Barye, and *The Serf*, to provide psychological stability at a time when his ideas on paintings were changing rapidly; he wanted the experience of physical volume, of actually making light and shade in an object, to supply him with an experience increasingly hard to recapture in painting once he had accepted the historical tendency towards flatness initiated by Impressionism. Finally, sculpture offered him at this time an area for the expression of feelings of a violence and intensity never to reappear so nakedly in his work. The first group of sculptures Matisse did, in the years 1899–1903, *The Jaguar, The Serf, Bust of an Old Woman, Study of a Foot, Horse, Ecorché, Madeleine I* and *II*, display a range of expressive subject and treatment unique in his art.

Matisse's sculpture has a mainly private function, especially at this time. I think it unlikely that he ever, even when engaged on *The Serf*, entertained the possibility of making a contribution to the tradition of monumental sculpture re-established by Rodin. All these early sculptures are of great and different interest, pointing to possibilities only a few of which Matisse was to realize, but all in various ways uneasy and incomplete in comparison with the fully achieved and daring pieces of the period from 1907. One notes among the early group the *Bust of an Old Woman*, with its slurred and greasy surface and strange forward lean in profile; but a subtle architectural energy from the piling-up of related forms on slightly displaced axes (foreshadowing the *Jeannette* series *III–IV*); the agitated surface of *The Serf*, the pose of which is so still (the relation with Rodin here seems more likely to me the studies for the *Balzac* rather than *The Walking Man*, as is generally assumed); and of the *Ecorché*, where the musculature is again transformed into sheer lumpiness –

88

77, 78 HENRI MATISSE *Bust of an Old Woman* 1900

79 HENRI MATISSE *Ecorché* 1903

80 HENRI MATISSE *Madeleine I* 1901

81 HENRI MATISSE *Joy of Living* 1905–06

82 HENRI MATISSE *The Dance* 1910

83 HENRI MATISSE *Music* 1910

contrasting with Brancusi's detailed and naturalistic treatment of the same subject.

By the time Matisse had worked through this first group of sculptures he had found his way in painting with the final release of colour from description in the Collioure landscapes of 1905. Simultaneously there occurred the vision of an ambitious and synthetic decorative art, drawing on his experience both of dealing with volume and the figure in sculpture and of the new possibilities opening up in the use of colour: *Luxe, calme et volupté*, 1904–05, *The Joy of Living*, 1905–06, *Luxury*, 1907, *Bathers with a Turtle*, 1908, *The Dance* and *Music*, 1910. Matisse clearly put his private struggle with sculpture to good use in this great succession of public and monumental painting; but the sculpture he made from 1907 onwards is itself as remarkable – notably the first *Reclining Figure*, whose pose originally comes out of these paintings, *The Serpentine*, and the *Two Negresses*, whose poses originated from photographs Matisse used when he had no model available at Collioure.[5] It seems significant to me that in all three of these great sculptures Matisse was working from a two-dimensional source which gave him total freedom to develop the sculpture in volume and disposition according to his own sense of the architecture of the parts. One notes also that in all these three pieces

84 HENRI MATISSE *Reclining Nude I* 1907

85 Henri Matisse *Two Negresses* 1908
86 Henri Matisse *The Serpentine* 1909

there is no problem of balance, the stability of each piece being assured by the horizontal pose, the locking of two figures, the supportive pillar. The legs, having no technically structural role, are freed to become equivalent in expressive power to the arms. The head becomes one in a series of lumps – shoulder, breast, buttock, calf. In each case the figure is unimportant except as a motif. The ferocity of expression randomly displayed in the earlier sculptures is concentrated into an expressive but quite abstract *theme* that characterizes each piece: in the *Reclining Figure*, an explosive diagonal thrust, in tension with the horizontality and relaxation of the pose; in the *Two Negresses*, the locking and interlacing of the figures at one level and the designing of the anatomy of both figures to reinforce this effect: in *The Serpentine*, the transformation of volume into line, so modulated as to re-invoke a volume of an entirely new order. Space itself is sucked into the sculpture, like air into a vacuum: space modelled, carved, stretched, compressed, with an energy corresponding to the stillness of the visual armature,

seen directly from front or back. Every inflection of the surface gives a key not only to a residual anatomic function, but affirms an outward, directional role, modulating the flow and pace of the surrounding void in favour of anti-anatomic, *perceptual*, rhythms and connections through the figure; contained and returned by the five 'windows' of space, the crucial apertures between left arm and head, right arm and back, between the upper legs and between the feet, and finally, the great central core of space framed by the continuous but varied structure of the left side of the figure, the base and the vertical support.

The heads of *Jeannette* of 1910–11 are often regarded as Matisse's sculptural masterpiece; and there are three aspects of the series which seem to me to have special significance.

Firstly, the connection of the *Jeannette* heads with Cubism: not that they can be said to derive from Picasso's *Head of a Woman* of 1909, a premature and superficial attempt to apply Cubism to sculpture, but that they demonstrate the liberating effect of Cubism on Matisse's sculpture. Picasso's and Braque's Cubism represented a more violent and total break with pictorial convention than anything that had happened since the Renaissance; the Impressionists, Cézanne, Seurat, Van Gogh and Gauguin, however radically they may have modified the structure of painting, still depended on a relation of artist to subject in which the former's role was fundamentally passive: that is to say he chose his subject and depicted his reactions to it, whether perceptual or expressive. Matisse, with his Fauve colleagues, freed colour from the subject and started to use it inventively and constructively: but the structure of the painting still remained that given by conventional perspective, the painter by implication sitting still and passive over and against the motif, receiving sensations and finding equivalents for them. By contrast, the Cubist painters were active in relation to their subject: they moved around it, as a sculptor would, and got to know it, in conceptual terms, as would an architect or engineer. The passive recipient of sensations became the active *maker*: this reversal of mental attitude long preceded its physical appearance in collage and construction. Its manifestation in pictorial terms was the breakdown of the picture surface into parts, units with individual identity but equal emphasis: the synthetic unity of single-point perspective was replaced by the structural coherence of the separate parts, re-unified in a new object.

This sudden access of power to the artist, received as an invitation to remake the physical world, explains the immediate and enormous influence of Cubism on the avant-garde in general. But within sculpture, to artists such as Brancusi and Matisse who had already evolved personal and original styles out of the elements of an existing convention, Cubism presented a challenge to the limits of that convention and a stimulus to make use of a new freedom. Each responded according to his temperament. Brancusi, turning from

87–91 Henry Matisse *Head of Jeannette I, II, III, IV, V* 1910–13

marble and limestone to wood, found a medium whose natural structural properties opened up the possibilities of an art more various, free and open than anything he had yet attempted. As for Matisse, I feel the *Jeannette* series is Cubist in inspiration, if wholly personal in development. It shows a development away from the conventional treatment of the head as a solid, unitary form with a continuously modelled surface; the emergence of parts which tend to threaten the closed unity of the whole, making it in effect an aggregation of lumps of contrasting character; and finally in *Jeannette V*, the invasion of the whole by the parts, so that although a homogeneous gestalt is re-established, the implied separation of the features penetrates to the core of the head. The total figure lends itself easily to the separation of its various components, and Matisse had already gone some way in this direction in the *Two Negresses* and the 1907 *Reclining Figure*; but to separate out the head – naturally the most unified and condensed of forms, as Brancusi was demonstrating – into virtually individual elements, was unprecedented, and must be accounted Matisse's most daring and original stroke in sculpture. Of course there were precedents in African carving, but only Matisse could have absorbed such a stylized and conceptual treatment of human features into his own perceptual and intuitive handling of form, in such a way as to resist the identification of any element of the whole except in terms of its belonging, its organic necessity in the development of the sculpture.

Secondly, the conception of the work in series. The sequence of heads is not carried out over a period of years, as with *The Back* reliefs, or with Brancusi's progressive refinement of his various motifs. The *Jeannette* series was made in the space of two years and worked on continuously during that period. The sculptures have a separate and individual character and presence, but they are part of a larger total, and gain from being seen together, as stages in a development. Matisse had previously painted separate 'states', progressive versions of a single subject, but never was the conception so ambitiously realized as in this series of sculptures.

The effect of the series is to mitigate the importance of the motif as such. The subject is not the woman's head, but the *process of making the woman's head*. The head is the vehicle of perceptual continuity, of recognition, no more. Elsewhere Matisse depicts the artist from behind in the act of painting the model, a more elaborate reflection of the same theme; the ambition of the *Jeannette* series is an indication of Matisse's confidence both in his own power and in the ability of sculpture to sustain so sophisticated a conception.

A third question raised by the *Jeannette* series is that of 'finish'. Here also Matisse was carrying out with greater concreteness solutions that he had found satisfying in painting. As the 'states' are somehow more separate and real when physically made, cast in bronze, than when depicted, so also is it more demonstrable in the nature of sculpture that a piece is finished, not

96

92–94 HENRI MATISSE
Henriette I, II, III 1925

95 HENRI MATISSE *Reclining Nude II* 1927

when it has achieved some imposed or stereotyped unity of style or surface, but simply when work on it has stopped, the artist has gone as far as he wants, and it is cast in bronze. The fact that Matisse in the *Jeannette* series and elsewhere used the plaster cast of an earlier state as an armature on which to continue modelling indicates the simultaneous presence of the aesthetic completeness of a certain stage and its provisional nature in face of the development of the series. Later Matisse was to make certain sculptures – *The Tiari, Henriette II*, for example – in which he achieved a tautness and smoothness of surface which approximate to a conventional idea of 'finish'. That this was only one possibility among many is shown by the fact that *Henriette II* is the second of a series in which the third and last, and most successful, returns to the area of modelling; the material is reasserted as soft, not hard, but the regularity and volumetric fullness of the second stage can be felt solid beneath the surface, giving the head a mysterious and subtle authority. The finish of both Rodin and Brancusi was accessible to Matisse, but he was committed only to the solution proper to the sculpture on which he was working.

This detachment from style, and from the lore of materials, gives Matisse's works a presence quite unlike that of Rodin's and Brancusi's. Volume for them is matter, hard or soft, a particular substance, whose natural character and resistance are contained in the conception and development of the work. Both, as sculptors trying to uncover what was central to a sculpture tradition,

96 Henri Matisse *Reclining Nude III* 1929

were primarily committed to realizing their feelings in terms of material and process. To Matisse, in contrast, a painter in search of a 'complete possession of his mind', the organization of volume was simply the proper concern of sculpture as that of colour was for painting. The experience of volume was thus essentially *abstract*: it initially derived from his eye and mind, not from the handling of material. The unequalled sensuousness of Matisse's use of clay should not be allowed to obscure the fact that his responses were perfectly controlled and deliberate.

The sculptures of Matisse that seem to me the most achieved and satisfying of his œuvre, the two reclining figures made in the late 1920s, raise certain questions about the nature of his ambition in sculpture. The pose of the figure forms an enclosed and contained unit; it can support itself without a base: the recumbent posture allows for a maximum of invention and distortion of shape without disruptive anatomical or structural consequences. Although the figure is at rest, there is a tremendous rotational movement inside the body; both shoulders and both knees are parallel to the horizontal, but there is a twist of 180° between them; pursuing the analogy in the second version, the forms of thighs and lower abdomen are transformed as if into two twisted strands of rope.

If one isolates the distinctive characteristics of these pieces – their contained overall shape, the habitual use of extended limbs as 'loops' containing and

97–98 Henri Matisse *The Back I c.* 1909; *The Back II c.* 1913–14

returning the movement within the figure, their relative smallness as objects, the pose being supported or at rest – one finds that they are typical of almost all the larger free-standing sculptures Matisse made after 1903. In general, these figures embody the same aim that he set himself in painting, that of conveying balance, harmony and order.

There is one category of pieces I have not yet touched on: those small heads and figures which were made in the hand, rather than on the modelling-stand. Here the presence of the hand creates not the surface but the form; in consequence they are not only intensely tactile but far less visually of a piece than the larger sculptures. They give one the feeling of having been squeezed into existence in a few moments rather than built up and trimmed down over long periods of work. The poses are often animated and unbalanced, and interact strongly with the surrounding space.

99–100 Henri Matisse *The Back III c.* 1914; *The Back IV c.* 1929

When one considers the polarity between these two modes in Matisse's sculpture, one becomes aware of the technical and aesthetic limits imposed by his major commitment to painting. That is to say, the larger, more composed pieces have a character and presence equivalent to that of easel paintings. Their relatively small size, their lack of aggression, their quality of contained and internal life, their balance and order, remove them from the real world, gives them a slightly remote, 'framed' character: one attends to them as one would to a view, or a painting. One feels that Matisse had neither the desire nor the technical capacity to make something more ambitious, more direct, out of the overt intensity and animation of the smaller, more tactile sculptures.

It is significant of Matisse's fundamental commitment as a painter that the one project of his that could be regarded as an attempt to make an ambitious monumental sculpture – *The Back* series – is in the form of relief. That is to say, they are one-sided like a painting, and though there is plainly more than one view from the front, the point of the relief form is that it works by *illusion*: that is, that the real and tangible form on the surface of the relief stands for a volume and displacement in depth that remain ambiguous. Matisse's use of the modelled relief form is almost unique in modern art of the first rank: and it is a splendid example of an acute awareness of limitations being turned spectacularly into a positive strength. Matisse was not interested in those technical and preliminary aspects of monumental sculpture that not only consume time and effort, but in fact tend to narrow and make rigid the sculptor's conception. He wanted the development of the work to be accessible to his control, and possibly radical modification, at all times. Rodin's flexibility was hard won, at the expense of years of craft experience, of banal dealing with matter and process. Matisse had the sensibility but not the equipment of a major sculptor, and his most ambitious effort in sculpture proper, this relief series, is enormously sculptural in feeling, but pictorial in effect: the tension between the two modes giving the series a somewhat ambiguous power. When one starts to consider how the figures in the various panels would work if they were fully realized in three dimensions, the imbalance of the first figure or the vast bulk of the last in the group makes it evident that Matisse's intensely felt working of volume is structured in terms of the vertical rectangle and its physical flatness or shallowness.

Matisse's central position in modern art was gained and sustained by his awareness of what he felt to be the proper and essential qualities of each branch of the plastic arts and his isolation and development of those qualities. In easel painting, in mural decoration, in drawing in various media, in sculpture, Matisse's attitude to each was in consideration of its *separateness*: each having its own tradition, its own means, its own effects, each demanding an attitude of mind, a working method proper to itself; the unifying factor consisting solely in the intuition and confidence of the artist. What is peculiar about the cut-outs in the context of Matisse's total work is that they were a new form, without history or precedent. He initially used cut paper shapes to assist in mural designs, then for the designs of tapestries, rugs, ceramics and stained glass. Many of the most ambitious cut-papers after 1950 were still designed to be executed in some other medium, or are conceived still in terms of large scale easel paintings, which strongly work against an enclosing rectangle, or of mural decorations which were clearly designed to be translated into ceramic and to animate a wall. But there is one group of cut-outs which are complete and satisfying in the original material and which need neither enclosing frame nor wall for support: and which may fairly be

102–104 Henri Matisse *Seated Blue Nude I, II, III, IV* 1952

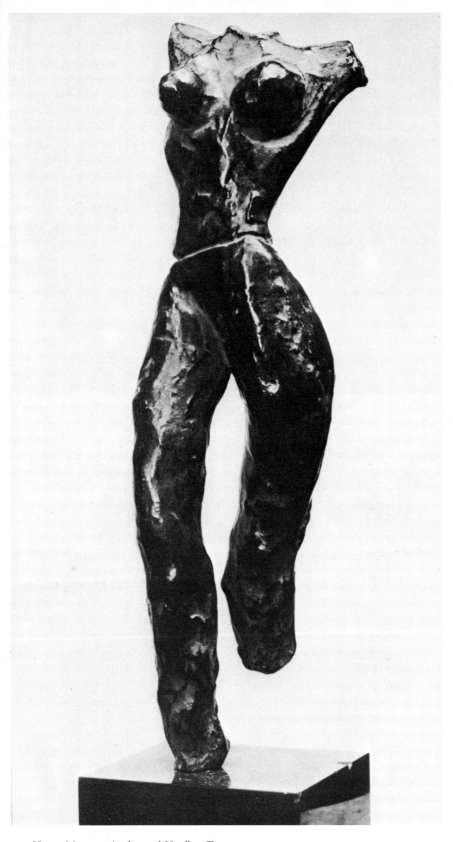

105 Henri Matisse *Armless and Headless Torso* 1909

106 Henri Matisse *Nude with Flowing Hair* 1952

considered a new order of sculpture – the great *Blue Nude* series which he completed in 1952.

The relationship of the poses of these figures with certain sculptures can easily be established – the seated nudes with the *Crouching Nude* sculptures of 1908, the *Nude with Flowing Hair* with the *Armless and Headless Torso* of 1909, the *Standing Blue Nude* with the *Upright Nude* of 1904, and *Torso with Head (La Vie)* of 1906, and so on: but this similarity of articulation is not surprising. What seems to me much more fundamental is a correspondence in freedom, even wildness, of handling between Matisse's less composed sculptures of the 1903–13 period and the cut-out figures: Matisse can accept the motif of figures in poses of abandoned emotion, even physical movement, and the static figures are imbued with an energy and restlessness that was ironed out of the more considered sculpture and paintings. The connection between the two consists in the directness of Matisse's relation with the material – clay formed in the hand, paper shapes formed by the action of scissors. In both cases Matisse was *in* the material and subject to it to a greater extent than his habitual detachment would allow elsewhere.

These cut-out nudes may be considered sculpture too in their unity of colour, and central coherence of shape. They follow from *The Back* reliefs in their acceptance of the condition of flatness as a basis for creating an illusion of volume that has no dependence on deep perspective. The drawing of the shapes, their apparent overlapping and entwining, contrast with a rigorous flatness and separation of form; the freedom and invention of proportions and postures, with the given articulation of the body. These figures, and notably the seated *Blue Nude* series, combine the serenity and order of the reclining figures of 1929 with the energy and abandon of the *Ecorché* and the painted figures in *The Dance* of 1910. They represent the point at which Matisse's potential greatness as a sculptor was realized in a form that carried the full range and power of his experience in art.

6   The Object

If one word captures the aspirations of modernism from about 1870 until the
Second World War, it is surely *object*. Firstly in poetry and painting, then in
sculpture, music and architecture, the world came to denote an ideal condition of self-contained, self-generating apartness for the work of art, with its
own rules, its own order, its own materials, independent of its maker, of its
audience and of the world in general. It is essentially a classic and optimistic
ideal, depending on a strong belief in the power and centrality of art in human
experience, and manifesting itself with the clarity and economy of scientific
law or engineering structure. The ideal of the object was enormously fruitful
in sculpture, and most notably in the period 1907–15. Subsequently the
accessibility of the ideal for sculpture created particular problems.

Sculpture, of its nature, *is* object, in the world, in a way in which painting,
music, poetry are not;[1] thus the ambition of the poem-object, the *objet-tableau*,
continued to be active over a far longer period than that of the sculpture-
object, because of the persistence of factors of meaning and representation in
poetry and painting. In fact the object-status of the poem or painting tended
to release and enlarge the evocations and associations in the component words
or depicted subject, whereas the effect in sculpture was the reverse: as the
sculpture-object approached the reality-object in form and intention, the gap
between them dwindled to the point at which all reasons for making
sculpture, and indeed art in general, seemed to disappear. This was the nature
of the crisis that was experienced by advanced art in the 1920s, when most
artists – including those who had been chiefly responsible in achieving the
success of 'the object' in sculpture and painting, Brancusi and Picasso –
seem to have felt an impulse to move backwards or forwards violently. It is
as though the position gained were incapable of steady development, but
demanded either the unconditional surrender of the conventions with which
they had been warring (but on whose existence their art had depended), or
counter-revolution.

If might be well to examine first the components of the drive towards the
object, because these were often in conflict. Out of, and in opposition to, the
subjectivity of early nineteenth-century Romanticism, came the objectivity

of naturalism – the affirmation of the objective world, and its precise and 'scientific' rendering. At its purest this tendency was represented by Impressionism, where landscape and light provided a neutral subject-matter: but in Flaubert, Baudelaire, Rodin, Rilke, exactness of rendering acted as the vehicle for the depiction of extreme states of feeling. Objectivity of perception allied to unusual, bizarre or 'degrading' subjects thus gave new life to Romanticism. I have already discussed Rodin's objectivity of *method*, his workmanlike physical approach to his art, which he shared with Flaubert and with the Impressionists. But, unlike the Impressionists, he himself could not achieve the indifferent, 'objective' approach to his subject that he recommended to Rilke.

Out of objective perception, objective method, developed the objective consideration of the work itself – its *own* demands issuing from its *own* objective existence – the flatness, bounded rectangularity, colour and tactility of the painting, the appearance of the printed poem on the page, with the simultaneous objective consideration of the conventions needed to support the illusion of space and volume in painting and meaning in poetry. Thus Cézanne and Mallarmé emerged as the leaders of a heroic struggle for the independence of painting and poetry as self-contained disciplines, which paradoxically involved the re-structuring of objectively verifiable conventions of perception and verbal usage – such as perspective and syntax – in the conflicting interests of the painting or poem as *itself* physically verifiable.

Sculpture had to wait until the emergence of Brancusi for a talent and ambition ready for the task. It was not simply a question of appropriating objective tendencies in painting, as Degas and Rosso had done, and as Picasso was shortly to do to such spectacular effect in his Cubist constructions. What was required, in addition to Rodin's objectivity of observation, was an objectivity of handling and subject-matter such as occurs only rarely in Rodin's œuvre – for example in the studies for the *Burghers of Calais* and the *Balzac*. Brancusi's student sculpture and early work in Paris demonstrates at once a faithfulness to appearance and a firm, taut, sure and naturalistic rendering of flesh that are far from Rodinian. In addition, through choice or circumstance, or both, his favoured mode is the portrait bust. (One characteristic Brancusi and Rodin did share was the intrinsic modesty of their immature work, the containment of ambition until, with the *Age of Bronze* and *The Prayer*, respectively, the time came for a major statement; and one wonders how far circumstance – the expectation that each had of earning a living from his craft solely – had in the formation of their separate ambitions.)

It is generally assumed that Rodin's main contribution to the emergence of 'the object' in sculpture lay in exhibiting intentionally dismembered figures and fragments as complete sculptures in themselves. There are several arguments that make me doubt this. In the first place, on Rodin's part, there

107 AUGUSTE RODIN *Large Head of Iris* 1891

is his own unsureness as to which of the vast accumulation of components stored in his studio were in themselves 'sculpture'. It is not that such of the fragments as have been cast and exhibited are not enormously impressive; rather that one is suspicious of an evidently wilful and random mode of selection and presentation. Moreover, the fragments, such as the justly celebrated *Iris* figures of 1890–91, still read as signs for figures; indeed, the evident purpose of truncation, from the *Walking Man* on, was to increase figural expressiveness, to increase the empathy of the spectator with the figure by forcing him to 'read' with his own body the missing parts of the sculpture. Seen purely as an abstract shape, if it is possible to do so again after making the figure reading, such a fragment as the *Flying Figure* has little character, order, or formal interest. That Rodin recognized, and put to use, this element of *recognition* as the sole factor in bringing order and expression out of sheer formlessness, is evidenced by the *Great Head of Iris*. However, here a new element obtrudes itself: truth to nature in representation is replaced by truth to the material, clay, presented in its essence as sheer passive inert *lump*.

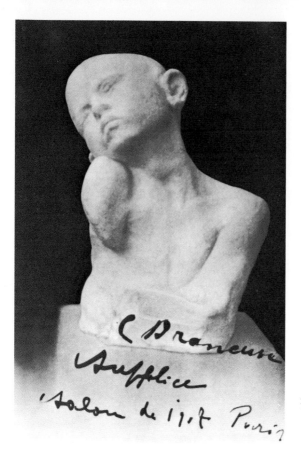

108 CONSTANTIN BRANCUSI
Torment I 1906

I have mentioned that Brancusi's earliest sculptures were largely portraits. We know that during his early years in Paris he continued to make life studies; so there are strong grounds for thinking that there were more than economic reasons for favouring the head as subject.[2] What must have appealed to Brancusi was the conventional and symmetrical containment of the portrait bust; and it was on the basis of this conventional form that Rodin's example in fragmenting the figure was useful to him, for example in the *asymmetrical* reduction of the limits of the conventional form. Here Brancusi's purpose evidently is at odds with Rodin: where Rodin's intention in truncating the figure is to call attention to the missing part, Brancusi's is the opposite – to concentrate what is there, to use the section to articulate the central solid. In the two versions of *Torment* from 1907, for example, Brancusi can be seen progressively moving from an expressive to an objective mode. In the first, the evocation of pain is created by the inclination of the head against the right shoulder; the face itself is expressionless; one does not question the position of the right arm cut off at the shoulder; the shoulder, bunched up against the side of the jaw, is a sufficient expressive focus. But the lower part of the chest and the left forearm are indeterminately realized, blurring the transition between the sculpture and the point at which it meets

109 CONSTANTIN
BRANCUSI *Torment II*
1907

the real world in a 'Rodinesque' fashion. In the second version Brancusi removes the artiness and indecisiveness of this lower section with a single clean cut, and the sculpture is instantly realized and transformed. There is no feeling that the body and left arm continue downwards, through the base – the effect that Brancusi was clearly guarding against in the first version. The upper part of the body now reads as a compact block, its mass horizontal against the diagonal axis of the neck and head. The proportions of each element, now clearly defined as shape, can be read against each other. The latent geometry of the conception is affirmed; and in the process, strangely, the communication of pathos is accentuated also. Nor does the preciseness of realization interfere with the emergent abstract structure of the piece: the axis through the protruding ears plays against the axis through the shoulders. The twist of the whole sculpture is even more evident in the beautifully modelled back, with its simple opposition of volumes.

The potential object-nature of Brancusi's early heads is evident not only through a backward reading of his later development, but through their small size, not apparent from reproduction; the detached heads of babies, for example, rest easily in the hand, and seem to invite this sort of response.

110 Constantin Brancusi *Sleeping Child* 1908

The clean horizontal section through *Torment II* also has the effect of precisely indicating the inclination of the head from the vertical. The *Sleeping Child* (cast in 1908, but probably modelled in 1906) is again convincingly complete in itself: the axis of the head, finding a 'natural' base on the cheek, conveys the subject with marvellous economy, while the exposed edge of the bronze cast at the neck affirms the sculpture's 'objectness' without disturbing the image.

The handling of the surface of this piece recalls Rodin, as does the undefined volume of rough marble surrounding *Sleep* of 1908. The device evidently stems from such Rodin pieces as *Thought* and *Aurora*, in which an exactly defined head emerges from a great lump of uncut marble. Rodin himself in these sculptures was quoting from Michelangelo's unfinished *Slaves*. Brancusi's purpose in employing this device was as plastic as Rodin's was literary. The rough marble around the head, suspending gravity, at once 'explains' its horizontal axis, and referring back to Michelangelo, makes the head's presence in the stone reasonable, in that there is a fair chance of its escape: the whole might fairly be seen as a work in progress. Indeed it was an early statement of Brancusi's 'egg' theme, whose most beautiful realization is

111 CONSTANTIN BRANCUSI
Sleep 1908

112 AUGUSTE RODIN *Aurora*
1885

113 CONSTANTIN BRANCUSI *Sleeping Muse* 1910

the bronze *Sleeping Muse* of 1910. This work is exactly poised between its condition as 'head' and its condition as 'object'. In contrast to Rodin's *Head of Iris*, which one has to *identify* as a head, one *knows* the *Sleeping Muse* is a head. So much is given, one does not question it. Thereafter one reads the features, the hair, the ears, their character and disposition – in their graphic shape *on* the surface, and in their varied but shallow articulation *of* the surface – as affirming and echoing the total and detached horizontal ovoid, the abstract form. Moreover the modelling of the form, its delicate but perceptible asymmetry, derives neither from its original condition as 'head', nor from the ideal egg-form to which it tends, but from its actual condition as 'object-head'; its horizontality being its prime character, affecting the gravitational distribution of mass within. The half-polished but still imperfect surface, the residual features and neck, contribute to its utter naturalness, its poise both as object and as image; neither aspect dominates. One feels that in later versions of the type, as the state of objectness became more accessible, Brancusi sought to rarefy the theme, to remove it from the everyday world of objects – to which of course the egg image familiarly belongs – by the immaculate surface and high reflective polish.

114

The *Beginning of the World* is the most extreme, most celebrated statement of this conception of the object; but although its proportions and its highly polished surface are far from mechanical, the achievement of objectness seems too easy, too complete. It has a theatrical presence which cannot replace the tension between the real and the invented that gives the *Sleeping Muse* its singular beauty.

The four *Cups* which Brancusi made in the years 1918–25 are the only sculptures in his œuvre which take an object rather than a person or animal as subject.[3] They are thus quite distinct from the useful objects, bases, studio furniture, and so forth which were made by Brancusi with the same tools and the same vocabulary of form, but which were clearly not intended for the same apprehension and scrutiny as the sculpture. The *Cup* is carved in wood and is much larger than its model in reality; it is solid, no longer a container, and the handle also is filled in; its underside is now a complete hemisphere, so that the top surface is tipped from the horizontal and tends to read as the sculpture's 'face'. It is an appealing object, with strong and simple proportions. To replace the living model, which seems to have been a vital stimulus for Brancusi, the artist has had to animate the sculpture, to give it something of the presence of one of his familiar animals and children: the translation of the cup from reality into sculpture has a kind of folklorish humour, a certain sentimentality.

Brancusi's *Cup* series, as a conscious attempt to make an object as sculpture, must owe something to that general concern with the object which emerged from Cubist collage. Here, in a far more public and dramatic form than in Brancusi's prolonged and isolated quest, the subject (still-life), the means of representation (elements of the real world) and the formal vehicle (the surface and boundary of the painting) were converging at such a rate that it seemed obvious to many of the followers, though not to the authors, of Cubism that if this pressure and this direction were to be sustained, both painting and representation were doomed, leaving the real world, or some aspect of it, as simultaneously subject and object for the artist. The period after the Russian Revolution and the ending of the First World War was one of almost hysterical optimism for the avant-garde, as if the whole world had been presented to them for reconstruction on the principles of Cubism. A Utopian vision of reality in effect replaced the conventional subject-matter of previous art. And on the pretext of a reconstruction of reality, and the declared rejection of all the familiar elements of traditional painting and sculpture, the range and vocabulary of sculpture was enormously enriched.

Duchamp, Tatlin, Rietveld and others, whatever their own beliefs as to the significance of what they were doing, produced objects which can now be seen to belong to modern sculpture, just as they themselves were embedded in and formed by the traditions they variously repudiated. The process of

115–118 CONSTANTIN BRANCUSI *Cup I, II, III, IV c.* 1918–25

reclaiming their work for sculpture has been protracted; and, as the career of Giacometti shows, the premature exploitation of their discoveries resulted in an ingenious but essentially sterile academicism. It is only in the last few years, when the proscription of all materials except wood, stone and bronze has finally been relaxed and sculpture has recovered a natural scale relationship with the human figure, that the potential of gestalt, scale, structure and material implicit in the work of these artists could be appreciated and used.

Duchamp's *Readymades* are elements of Cubist still-life released from the medium of painting. There are inevitable difficulties with these pieces, such as the problem of being unable to see them except in photographs or in the inferior multiple copies that Duchamp released at the end of his life. Certainly, Duchamp's proclaimed attitude towards these works, the uninspired character of most of his subsequent work, and the use to which the *Readymades* have been put, justifying a flood of feeble imitations, must all add up to a pretty strong case against taking the originals seriously.

Yet I was enormously affected by the image of the *Bottle Rack* when I first saw it *as sculpture*, however it came into existence and whatever its history and exploitation, and I find that I still am. The same holds true for the urinal, the snow shovel, the hat rack. By comparison, the rest of Duchamp's work,

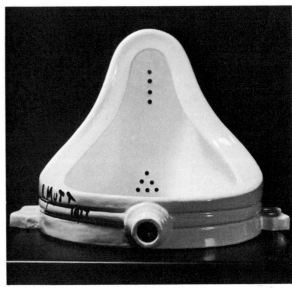

119 MARCEL DUCHAMP *In Advance of the Broken Arm* 1915 (1945)

120 MARCEL DUCHAMP *Fountain* 1917 (1938)

121 MARCEL DUCHAMP *Bottle Rack* 1914 (1964)

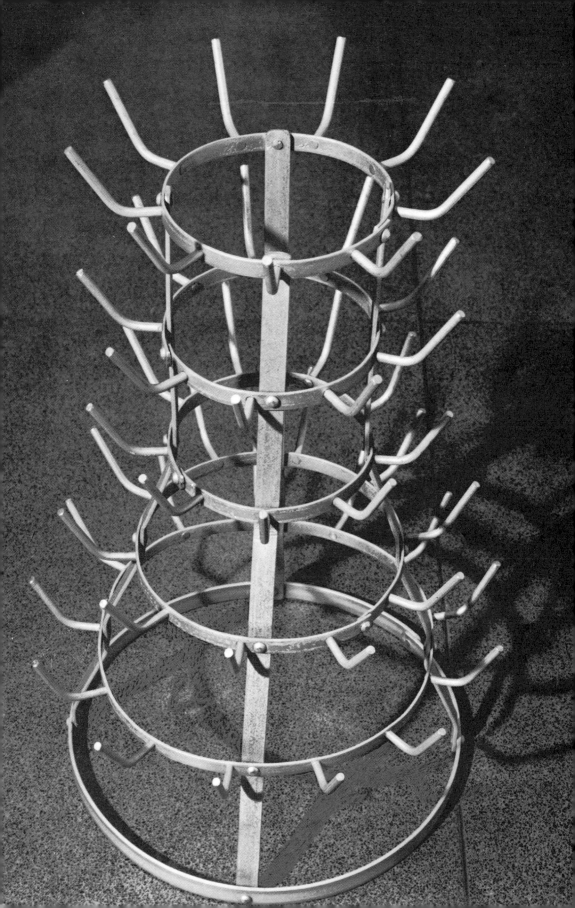

122 MARCEL DUCHAMP *Hat Rack*
1917 (1964)

before and after, seems contrived, over-elaborate, clever, whimsical, mechanical and boring. The *Bottle Rack* and the other pieces I mentioned are inspired: they do not work simply on their incongruity, as useful objects in an art context; in fact their detachment from the original context, except with the snow shovel, makes them virtually unrecognizable *except as sculpture*, i.e. in terms of their abstract properties – image, proportion, structure and use of material. This is the inversion of Duchamp's professed intention to make art unnecessary by substituting common, mass-produced objects for art objects. However, the whole enterprise depended on the general cultural structure built around the making and appreciation of art, the needs it satisfies and the expectations it creates. Duchamp could not escape being part of this structure, and while in the short term his betrayal of his own talent may have diminished art, I am convinced that the effect of his best work will in the end be seen to have enlarged it. The *Readymades* witness how Duchamp, his taste and sensibility sharpened by the competitiveness of Cubist Paris, where he had arrived too late for his contribution to be anything but academic, found in exile in New York mechanically fabricated objects whose completeness, simplicity and order must have seemed but a step from the stripped and dismembered bottles, glasses and guitars of Braque and Picasso's collages of 1912–15. The formal integrity which these

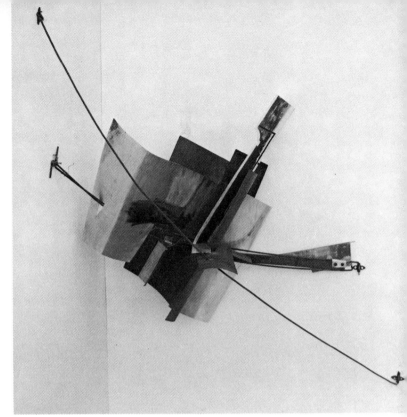

123 VLADIMIR TATLIN *Corner Relief* 1915

objects possess is typical of a great number of useful objects in general circulation in the nineteenth century where function, economy and efficiency had been the only determinants of design. It was Duchamp's achievement, in spite of himself, to bring this whole area of form and use of materials into sculpture, where subsequently it has been untapped, except in the work of David Smith, who was the first to incorporate tools and machine parts into sculpture for their abstract rather than image quality. However the abstract formal power of the *Bottle Rack* as a total configuration is still unequalled in sculpture.

Vladimir Tatlin's career offers a strange parallel to Duchamp's, and as with Duchamp his most important work is not available except in photographs or reconstructions. As with Duchamp, this is largely due to the artist's desire to move the object beyond the context where it could be received and appreciated as art. In contrast to Duchamp, however, Tatlin always affirmed the primacy of aesthetic considerations in all his projects.

Tatlin's aesthetic, his 'culture of materials', derives from Cubist collage, from the period of his stay with Picasso in Paris (1913). The straight and curved lines and planes representing the elements of Cubist still-life are transformed in Tatlin's reliefs of 1914–17 into the 'functional' forms of real materials. Steel and aluminium sheet, flat, rolled, or profile-cut; sawn,

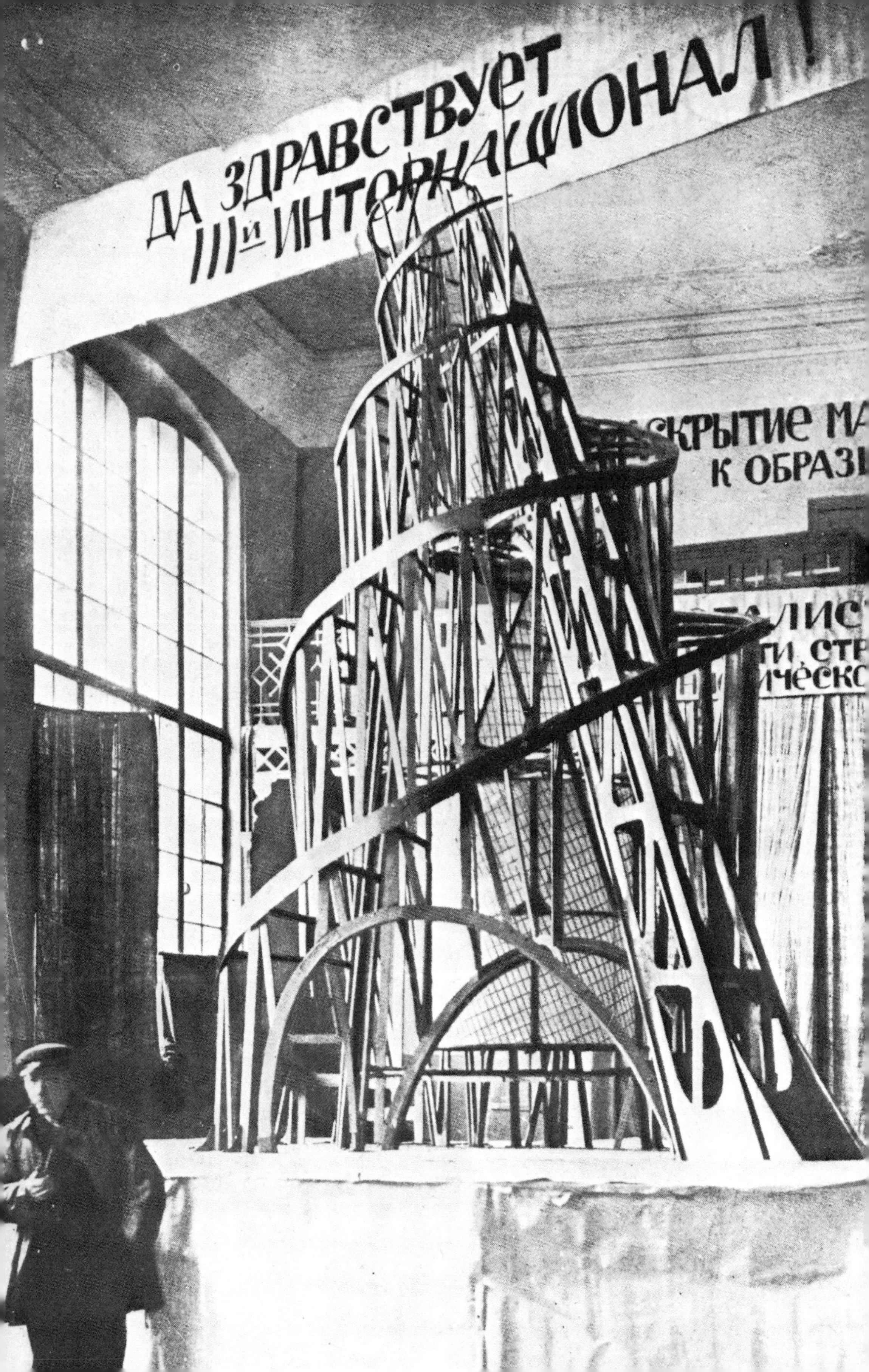
ДА ЗДРАВСТВУЕТ
IIIй ИНТЕРНАЦИОНАЛ!

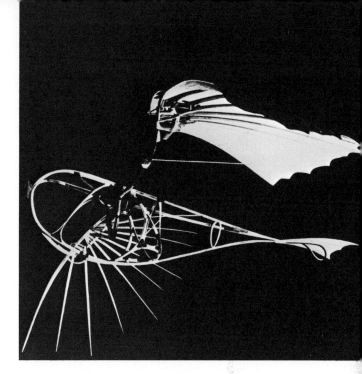

124 Vladimir Tatlin *Monument to the Third International* 1919–20 (model)

125 Vladimir Tatlin *Letatlin* c. 1932

planed, drilled sections of wood; wire bent in curves, cables under tension; other materials including glass and string; all are tautly and dynamically organized in structures which appear to thrust into the spectator's own space. Until the Soviet authorities are prepared to release Tatlin's surviving work, one can only guess at the quality of these reliefs: but my guess is that they will prove to be very good indeed.

Tatlin's *Monument to the Third International* was his first fully free-standing structure. In spite of its grandiose intention (the final version was to be 400 metres high) its form seems to have largely resulted from the materials – wood with steel brackets – from which he constructed the original model. Disregarding its total impracticability as engineering structure, and considering the model purely on aesthetic grounds, it is undoubtedly an impressive object, wild, generous, and energetic, with a surprising variety of views. But it has the faults of these virtues – there is much in it that seems redundant, capricious or merely confused. It is a flawed structure because Tatlin seems to have been unable to decide whether he was making a model or the real thing. Its character, like that of so much Russian Constructivist work, is closer to stage design than to sculpture, or architectural engineering.

During the 1920s Tatlin moved from the design of prototype use-objects – a chair, a stove, a suit of clothes, etc. – to the design of an ornithopter, or air bicycle, *Letatlin* (Russian *letat'*, 'to fly'). What led him to this was, typically, an aesthetic motive – the desire to find an ordered and rational structure based entirely on curves. A flying machine would at once give form and purpose to

123

his aesthetic beliefs, while realizing the fantasies of dynamism and release which the *Monument* merely symbolized. 'I have made it as an artist. Look at the bent wings. We believe them to be aesthetically perfect. Or don't you think *Letatlin* gives an impression of aesthetic perfection?'[4] The skeleton of the ornithopter is indeed a beautiful structure, so far as one can gather from photographs. In contrast to the *Monument* the materials were selected and worked with the greatest care and precision: steamed and bent wood; 'ash, linden, willow, cork, silk ropes, aluminium and even white-tanned leather'.[5] The aesthetics were perfect, but the dream of an air bicycle for the masses was unrealized. The remainder of Tatlin's career is one of the most depressing episodes in the history of modern art. However, the fruits of Tatlin's work, especially in his investigation of the form-giving properties of materials not previously considered worthy of sculpture, remain available to us.

'The so-called red-blue chair, the chair made of two boards and a number of laths, that chair was made to the end of showing that a thing of beauty, i.e. a spatial object, could be made of nothing but straight, machined materials. So I had the plank sawn into strips and laths; the centre part I sawed in two halves, so I had a seat and a back and then, with the laths of various lengths, I constructed the chair. When making that thing, it never occurred to me that it would prove to be all that meaningful for myself and possibly for others too' (Gerrit Rietveld, in a filmed interview).[6] Rietveld was brought up in his father's furniture workshop as a designer and maker of objects. As

126 GERRIT THOMAS RIETVELD *Red-Blue Chair (Unpainted)* 1918

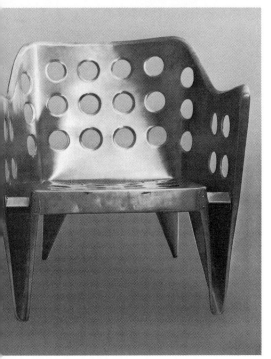

GERRIT THOMAS RIETVELD *Aluminium Chair* 1942

128 GERRIT THOMAS RIETVELD *Chair with Leather Straps and Steel Frame* 1927

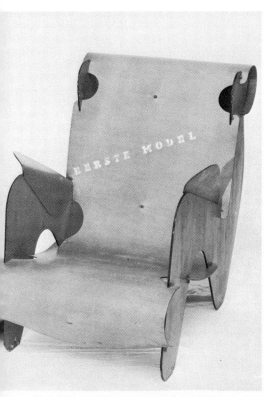

129 GERRIT THOMAS RIETVELD *Plywood Chair* 1927

an architect and an early member of De Stijl, he was in a position to put into practice the dreams of remaking the world that animated the post-war avant-garde. His Schröder House in Utrecht (1924) is a key piece in the evolution of the modern movement in architecture, and the first building in which De Stijl theory was realized, just as the red-blue chair (1918) had been the first embodiment of De Stijl in three dimensions. However, the chair exists in an earlier, unpainted version, in which its material and construction are more positively affirmed; and what binds Rietveld to Duchamp and Tatlin in the development of the object in this period is the great series of chairs he made largely during the 1920s, which are virtually abstract structures articulating the simplest and most expressive ordering of materials within the general concept of 'chair'.

They do not seem intended primarily for use or for production; they exist as autonomous chair-objects, conceived and elaborated for their own sake.[7] Wood in rectangular and round sections, bent and moulded plywood and fibreboard, steel tube, sheet aluminium and plastic are employed separately or in various combinations. There is no repetition. Each chair is a new adventure. The sensitivity to the aesthetic properties of 'ordinary' materials, the invention in joining rigid materials and bending and forming flexible materials to give structural strength, the sense of detail and proportion, give these pieces a character and an authority which attach them to the history of modern sculpture. Rietveld's own ingenuous description – 'a thing of beauty, i.e. a spatial object' – should alone leave no doubt that here an artist, rather than an architect, designer or craftsman, was at work. Indeed, it is evident, from Rietveld's own evolution as an increasingly successful architect, that as his distance from the work increases, when invention is no longer taking place in and with tools and materials, the product declines into an anonymous 'modernity'.

Though he made other objects of extraordinary force and beauty – for example the celebrated sideboard (1919), and the suspended lamp of three opposed fluorescent tubes – the chair seems to have long been Rietveld's central preoccupation and certainly the area in which he achieved the most consistent success. Its size, its relation to the human form and to the ground, its necessary strength, its relation to gravity both in its own structure and its supportive role, its stressed horizontality and verticality, its separation of inside and outside, front and back – all these factors make the chair an analogy for the human figure as well as a useful object. For Rietveld, the chair was evidently 'subject' rather than object, as the figure was 'subject' for Rodin.

Rietveld's chairs, together with Duchamp's *Readymades* and Tatlin's useful objects and glider, demonstrate how the object had itself become subject: that it was in the end the quality of the artist's eye, hand and mind, that would distinguish his object from other things and from reality in general.

126

However, because of the attitudes of these artists – the proclaimed anti-art stance of Duchamp and Tatlin, and the self-effacement of Rietveld – and the conventions of appreciation of sculpture, most of the attention and credit for the realization of the object in sculpture has gone to Giacometti, who had less of a sense of sculpture than any of these three, but a far greater sense of the moment, of how much and what taste in sculpture could take in the late 1920s and 1930s.

Giacometti's sensibility was always, as his post-war figurative style demonstrates, that of a painter. Most of his pre-1930 sculptures are either frontal and planar, or laid out on the horizontal as a tableau. The object of which he made a slogan – 'objects without pedestals and without value, be thrown away' – became in his hands essentially an academic concept: the sculpture-object of Brancusi, the objects of Cubist still-life, the objects of Duchamp, are re-incorporated into sculpture in traditional materials, plaster, bronze and wood. The ingenuity of his borrowing and juxtaposition, and the clarity of his presentation, cannot conceal the fundamental lack of feeling.

It is more an indication of sculpture's poverty than of Giacometti's talent that his work has acquired such a reputation. And even now that his post-war figures are coming to be recognized for what they are – the tiresome and inflated repetition of a single idea (the articulation of form by perception), which had already been used to far greater effect by Matisse – the early sculptures have acquired a niche in the history of modernism that has seemed impregnable. But the more one looks at these early pieces, the more suspect their quality becomes. Only one sculpture, the *Woman with her Throat Cut*, communicates a real and authoritative coincidence of image, formal invention, and handling of material. Elsewhere the object world is exploited for its contained gestalts, simple and symmetrical structure and mechanical forms: but the deadness of the handling, the slackness of the proportions, only serve to emphasize the dependence of the sculptures on imported figurative and intellectual referents.

7 Brancusi at Tîrgu Jiu

Brancusi's most ambitious sculptures, *The Endless Column*, *The Gate of the Kiss*, and *The Table of Silence*, are situated in the town of Tîrgu Jiu in the south-west of Romania, where they were erected in 1937–38. The sculptures are aligned along a mile-long axis across the town, with the *Table* at its western limit adjoining the River Jiu and the *Gate* at about 150 yards distance along a broad path flanked by woodland (both sculptures are in the public park); the *Column* is at the other end of the town, with streets and the church of the Holy Apostles intervening between it and the other pieces, from which it is not visible. Finally, there is a smaller version of the *Table*, without stools, about 200 yards beyond the *Column* itself, which stands in a large rectangle of scrubby parkland rising slightly away from the town, traversed by gravel paths laid out in an obtrusive radial symmetry, dotted with small trees, and bordered by occasional low houses. Neither the sculptures themselves nor the plan on which they are laid out are immediately apparent to the visitor to the town: only the *Column*, which is nearly 100 feet high, can be seen from any distance.

The present physical condition of the sculptures and their immediate surroundings bears witness to their problematic character as public art. The *Table* and *Gate*, located in a physically pleasant and much-used place of recreation, seem to be well looked after. The *Table* has always had a symbolic rather than a real function. The *Gate* is used, in the sense that, being set back a few yards from the entrance to the park, people have the choice to walk through it or around it. While they do both, I never observed anyone actually looking *at* the great obstruction in their path. At all events, both sculptures, together with a number of stone stools, benches, and so on, which Brancusi designed, are accepted as decorative elements in a public place, whose power as art, the capacity to surprise and disturb, has been drained off by habit and implied function.

The *Endless Column*, however, stands in an open space that has no other purpose than to set it off. The sculpture itself now leans off the vertical, and the original bright gilt finish has discoloured to the tone of dark bronze or wood.[1] One's first impression of the *Column* in its own area is that it is neglected and unwanted; its substantiality, in terms of fame, and physical mass and engineering achievement, is evidently more of an embarrassment than an asset to the town. The sculpture has the air of being rarely visited, either by the local people, who would have no reason to go there but to look at it, or by tourists, for whom it is depicted in glossy brochures as one of the attractions of Romania together with churches, castles, and historic ruins; or by those artists and art writers from the West, by whom it has been so frequently cited and discussed in recent years, when this particular work has assumed the character of a talisman. Nonetheless, the bleakness, even hostility, of its surroundings present the sculpture to the visitor without distraction or subterfuge, charm or excuse. I for one have no doubt that the *Endless Column* emerges from this test, confronting one by the plain facts of its physical existence, and stripped of the mythmaking of Brancusi's disciples, and the misrepresentation of much recent propagandist writing, as a very great sculpture; the ambition of its size being a function of its conception, and no mere display of rhetoric.

The circumstances under which these sculptures came into existence are now of no more than historical interest. Curiously enough, the initial project at Tîrgu Jiu was for a war memorial, celebrating the resistance of the town to the Germans in 1917; the commission was passed on to Brancusi in recognition of his increasing fame in Western Europe and America, the sculptor virtually being given a free hand to build three monuments from his own vocabulary of motifs, in the town in which he had worked when as a child of nine he first ran away from his native village. During his long exile in Paris, Brancusi had maintained contact with his homeland and its artistic life; he was helped to survive during his penurious early years by portrait commissions from fellow countrymen. The single most crucial sculpture of the pre-war period, *The Prayer*, was the result of a commission for a funerary monument in Romania; and he continued to send sculptures back to Bucharest for the annual exhibition of the Tinerimea Artistică (the advanced wing of Romanian art) from 1907 until 1914.

After the First World War, when Brancusi's international reputation was established and his style and confidence were assured, he began to reach out for new problems. The struggle with representation no longer obtruded itself into the graceful and synthetic emblems he found for portrait heads, birds and fish. During the 1920s Brancusi sometimes conceded to, sometimes fought, his own facility. In general, during this period, the early rigour and awkwardness (for example, of *The Prayer*, the first *Kiss*) are more often displayed in the wood carvings and the bases than in the bronze and marble sculptures. The first *Endless Column*, the conception of which derives from earlier bases, was made in 1918, as was the later dismantled *Architectural Project*. Both pieces signal the challenge of an alternative road for sculpture –

lean, wholly abstract, and 'architectural' in a concrete rather than an ideal sense. Over this period, also, Brancusi played with the idea of a more literal and more decorative architecture; the projected *Temple of Love*, like the later and also unrealized *Temple of Meditation*,[2] was probably a structure to house objects, rather than in architecture in the sense which the Tîrgu Jiu group was to assume.

Thus the early 1930s found Brancusi looking for the opportunity to extend the reduction and refinement of the *Birds* into a more public, less protected realm, with possible models in the *Endless Column* and various bases; yet with a persisting desire to make his vision public by creating a specialized and theatrical viewing place around it, in effect a designed and idealized 'studio'. Perhaps we should be thankful that this dream of Brancusi's remained un-realized, or at least that the commission at Tîrgu Jiu evoked a response of nerve – drawing on the experience of thirty-odd years of making sculptures conceived and executed from hand size to life size, to be experienced within the limits of human scale, of the implied grasp and touch of hands, and of the intimate proximity to a portrait head, or one's reflection in a mirror.

Rodin, who struggled all his working life to make a morally engaged and edifying public art on the grand scale, achieved little in his great projects, each one in varying degrees frustrated, flawed and incomplete. Brancusi, by contrast, after virtually perfecting an ideal of sculpture that was the antithesis of Rodin's – private, silent, withdrawn, morally neutral – was to put at risk this whole achievement in the realization of public sculpture on a gigantic scale not attempted in his time by advanced artists of serious pretensions. The *Table* is 7 feet, the whole ensemble with stools about 18 feet in diameter; the *Gate* is over 17 feet high, 21 feet across, and 6 feet deep, and the mass of the lintel is enormous; the *Column* is 96 feet high, each of the 15 complete elements being the height of a man.

And yet none of the three sculptures at Tîrgu Jiu appears even large, and certainly they do not dominate or diminish the spectator (photographs, especially of the *Gate*, are most misleading in this respect). Brancusi is reported as saying that the spectator should not be made to feel like an atom in the presence of a work of art. Whether by organizing factors of distance, perspective, and existent elements in the environment, or through the drawing, disposition or proportions of the sculptures themselves, Brancusi achieves at Tîrgu Jiu that intimacy of the spectator with the single object that would seem possible only in the charged and cloistered ambience of the studio. It is possible that the sculptures are *so* large that their absolute size, in relation to human scale, is neutralized, and that they take on a dominantly optical rather than a physical character, through the absence of tactile referents. But this extraordinary effect of privateness, of intimacy, is brought about largely, I feel, by their character as *objects*. Their abstraction (though

132 CONSTANTIN BRANCUSI *Table of Silence* 1937

this varies in degree from piece to piece), their symmetry and completeness of gestalt, their strangeness (the physical presence belies the facile attribution of Brancusi's sculpture to Romanian folk art) – all these factors tend to isolate and distance them from the environment, to which they are otherwise so nicely adjusted.

It is a remarkable achievement, especially in view of the changes that time and nature have brought about, even in the last twenty-five years. However, it is an achievement of skill, rather than of art, and it is as art that the three pieces at Tîrgu Jiu must separately be evaluated.

The *Table* and the *Gate* form a group, in a common area, and may be considered quite apart from the *Column*. It is true that there is a continuous relation along the line down which all three sculptures are placed from *Table*, through *Gate*, to *Column*; between ground and sky, between horizontality and verticality, from massiveness to lightness, from opacity to transparency. But these graded relations arrive from a study of the design, rather than of the objects themselves; and the objects, even within the public park,

132

strongly assert their separateness. The *Gate* is visible from the *Table* only as a small white silhouette; the *Table* is virtually invisible from the *Gate*. Of the three pieces, the *Table* has to be seen from close to, for the ellipses of the top surfaces to read at all, and this effect of concealment of the piece from a distance is emphasized by its placing on a slight incline when approached from the *Gate*.

The *Table* is by far the least satisfactory of the sculptures at Tîrgu Jiu; its low elevation submerges it in the accidental distractions of the environment, while the horizontal top surfaces of both table and stools render them liable to be obscured by the contingencies of weather, and any deviations from the horizontal plane become very noticeable; the ground under some of the stools has subsided, disturbing the simple symmetry that is the main feature of the sculpture's composition. Even allowing for these accidents, and considering the piece purely as sculpture, I find a certain deadness, an inertia, a withdrawal from the highest standards implicit in Brancusi's art, both in the conception of the piece and in its internal proportions and relations. The squat massiveness of the table does carry an authority, but it is the authority of a 'good' and artless found-object, a millstone or whatever. The design of the stools again seems 'good'; but in *design* terms – that is, not the product of a wholly sculptural inspiration (the presence of variant stools of the same conception, but square instead of round in section, on either side of the path nearby, reinforces this impression). The placing of the twelve stools around the table, the distance between the stools themselves, and the stools and the table, also seems unhappy (though there is apparently a doubt here as to whether Brancusi's intentions as to the grouping of the stools were correctly carried out).[3]

In all, it is a sentimental piece, whose character verges on self-parody. That severe line which Sidney Geist has drawn to separate Brancusi's sculpture from the bases, furniture and useful objects reflects a clear division which the sculptor himself almost always respected. On the one hand, the sculptures proper – often, if not always, banal and awkward in the initial idea, but worked on and persistently defined by the carving process, in the individual piece and in series protracted and advanced over many years. On the other hand, the bases, and more notably the studio furniture, whose forms had been made possible by the innovations of the sculpture, but which are essentially objects of taste, whose formal character is circumscribed by their function. They set the tone, create the atmosphere of the studio, but they are not sculpture, and were not subject to the intensity of commitment to the risks and adventure that the sculpture carries. The *Table of Silence* at Tîrgu Jiu seems to me to be such an article of studio furniture, and its ambivalent status between art and taste cannot be redeemed by the portentous title and the dressing of symbolism. The idea of 'table' inhibits the growth of the object as

134 CONSTANTIN BRANCUSI *Leda* 1923

sculpture in inverse proportion as the idea of 'chair' unleashed truly sculptural invention in the 'craftsman' Rietveld. It may be that the *Table's* inclusion in the Tîrgu Jiu group at all resulted less from Brancusi's desire to realize this conception in itself as from his need to tidy up the vast project, to unify the other two pieces by providing a third term to the equation. The decorative symmetry of the pathway and the lining-up of the sculptures also seem directed to this end, giving what are essentially strange, aggressive and self-referring objects with their own 'pull' a 'place' as elements of formalized landscape.

In contrast with the disappointing effect made by the *Table*, the *Gate* is superb. It is as fresh as the first *Kiss*, and its simple structure represents as great an advance in the history of the *Kiss* motif as when the original statement seemed to arrive 'from nowhere' in 1907, in a manner unique in Brancusi's œuvre. All the reservations one might have had about the *Gate*

135

from acquaintance with it in photographic form fall away on confronting the real thing. In reproduction, the image of the sculpture evokes the classical triumphal arch, Oriental free-standing gateways, megalithic dolmens, and so on; but in reality the sculpture *feels* like none of these possible examples. To start with, it is marvellously light and airy: the actuality of the evident size and weight of the three component elements is countered by the proportions, the drawing of and on the sculpture, and the near-white colour of the stone; the great lintel seems to float over the columns and the central void, apparently anchored only at the points on either side where the deeply-incised circle around the eyes just clears the horizontal at the top centre of each column. The sculpture has an immensely warm and friendly presence: its effect is to draw in and embrace the spectator, who feels rather protected than oppressed by its great bulk.

The image of the *Kiss* is thus transformed from a description, however schematic, of two embracing lovers into a structure whose mass embraces the spectator and the spectator's space. The most spectacular distinction from the *Kiss* of 1907 is the way in which the block in which the original was carved has been replaced by the central space, a block of air, around which the gate is structured. The proportions of this central void, slightly higher than it is wide, echo the proportions, seen in profile, of that first *Kiss*. In the case of the *Gate*, the relation of this just-vertical central rectangle of space to the more emphatic horizontal rectangle of the external profile, is crucial to the effect of lightness.

The emphasis and proportions of the incised *Kiss* motif on the columns and lintel have become quite abstract and generalized, and the design is not immediately appreciable as depicted figures. Their function is to articulate, to carry the load of the sculpture: the drawing is most deeply incised, even modelled, in the centre of each column; the repeat motif carries the eye easily across the lintel, with its precisely etched incision; and at the top of the lintel, just under the coping, the drawing of the eyes and hair is just perceptible (as is the vertical line between the embracing lovers). The drawing thus tends to become lighter as the eye moves up the sculpture, and from the centre to the corners of the columns. This effect is heightened by the slightest of projections of the lintel over the columns, and the coping-stone over the lintel – just enough to counteract the inward lean induced by perspective as the sculpture moves upward from eye level.

Unlike the *Table*, the *Gate* has no longer to be read as a use-object. It is the true successor to Brancusi's first authentically modern sculpture, the conclusion to thirty years' continuous exploration of the rectangular block as the appropriate form for stone; the fundamental predictability, the obviousness, of the structure is balanced by the simultaneous awkwardness and subtlety of the proportion and drawing. Nothing has been taken for granted; the

135 CONSTANTIN BRANCUSI *Gate of the Kiss* 1937

'classical' theme, the enormous scale, have been tested and re-achieved with a total innocence and a naïve cunning. It implicitly challenges Rodin's *Gate of Hell*, opposing the incoherence and physical impenetrability of that unfinished project with its formal simplicity, its enclosing warmth and serenity, and its precise physical realization. It is a beautiful sculpture.

The *Endless Column* is better still. The sole theme in Brancusi's œuvre to have been abstract from its inception, it retrospectively seems destined for its final scale and location at Tîrgu Jiu. Earlier essays, such as the fragments in the Brancusi studio in the Musée d'Art Moderne in Paris, now appear incomplete and unachieved – and also too real, too graspable. The *Endless Column* motif first appears as a base. Whereas the table motif also served as a base for several of the larger horizontal sculptures of the 1920s, the *Column* early achieved an independent existence as sculpture (1918), and as outdoor sculpture – the piece in Steichen's garden (1920). The first try exists now only in Steichen's remarkable photographs, in which, however, the problem of how to suggest the 'endless' within the structure of the sculpture is evaded by obscuring both ends of the piece. While the success of this first sculpture will forever remain uncertain, Brancusi continued to make versions of it, testing its scale, modelling and proportions, until the time came for its definitive realization. Unlike the *Kiss*, the *Birds*, or other major themes, there is little redefinition of the image, given the initial (and wholly original) concept of the repeated invariable unit. Those qualities of random articulation, of density, of illusion, which are achieved through the relatively complex structure and handling of all his other sculpture, could be achieved on the larger scale only by perspective. The enormous dimensions of the Tîrgu Jiu column are the necessary condition of the sculpture's primarily optical existence. The module is virtually the height of a man: but from there its relation to human proportion has no significance. It is the relation to the human eye which is all-important, and from a few paces away, one's eye-level corresponds to the junction of the incomplete base element with the first complete element above it.

The sculpture starts at eye level; because of this fundamental principle no two elements can ever read as exactly identical, and to this fact too the sculpture owes its peculiar presence, appearing to be suspended as if hovering between earth and sky, seeming merely to touch the ground at the base.

Brancusi precisely calculated the nature and quantity of the viewing space for each piece at Tîrgu Jiu. The clear area on all sides of the *Endless Column* is large, a rectangle with a side of perhaps 300 yards, allowing a long view and a long approach to the sculpture. Because of this, and because there are no other features by which one can readily estimate its size, and because the proportions of the whole sculpture are light and slender, the actual size of the piece remains continually in question. It comes as a shock to see a man standing at the base, registering the real size of the sculpture, which otherwise reads as having no size, neither large nor small, simply as though a specific size was not one of its physical attributes. This is a major aspect of the sculpture's opticality: it is too large to be grasped, or measured against human scale, yet it can be seen from a distance which considerably diminishes it – indeed, in order to be taken in totally, without moving the field of vision, it *has* to be seen from this distance.

The *Column* comprises fifteen complete and identical elements, with a two-thirds element at the base, and a half element at the top. The lowest element is so shaped that there is no return taper after the widest point is reached about two feet above ground-level; the effect is physically and visually to lock and stabilize the sculpture as it meets the ground. Strangely,

138

it is hard at first to recognize the difference between the lowest element and the remainder. How the sculpture starts and finishes is plainly crucial to its success: here a lesser artist might have betrayed a magnificent conception, but Brancusi's attention over the years to the dynamics of this particular structure enabled him to lay hold of exactly the right solution, here as in the modelling and proportion of the element, and in the number of the units – too many to be visually comprehended without counting, yet few enough to read as a finite number.

The impermanence of the original gilt finish on the *Column* was the only serious miscalculation made by Brancusi at Tîrgu Jiu. Although the sculpture was never polished to a mirror-like finish like that of the bronze *Birds in Space*, it must have been intensely light-reflective when first executed, and the difference in its expressive character from its present state must have been substantial. The finish is now an uneven dull brown, with the third, fourth and fifth elements from the bottom still hinting at their former brightness. The combination of the present dark colour with the extended but regular proportions of the piece give it the feeling of wood. This is not inappropriate, considering that wood was the material in which the theme was first conceived, and from which Brancusi carved the original module of the Tîrgu Jiu *Column*.[4] Nor is there any sense in which the sculpture itself feels 'wrong' now: the dark finish seems so natural that the original might appear forced and theatrical to present taste.

The dark, wooden quality of the sculpture on first acquaintance gives it an 'African' character, which impression is reinforced by the optical effect of the light eating into the flat top of the highest half-element, recalling the scalloped crown of *King of Kings*. 'Marvellous is the fact that the elements of the *Column* do not diminish in size as they mount. The persistence of size and of shape, the constancy of the repetition, causes the *Column* to remain near to the mind as it moves off from the eye. We have here a poetry of the actual, without illusion or compensation, without tapering or entasis', writes Sidney Geist.[5] The optical performance of the *Endless Column* is stunning. The constancy which Geist describes is, of course, an illusion: the elements do not *appear* to diminish. What happens is that as the sculpture moves upward, away from the eye, the proportions of each element progressively become more squat, the breadth increasing proportionately to the height; the relative proportion of the lowest full element is 2:1, height to breadth, of the highest full element, possibly 1:1. Of course there has been an *absolute* perspective contraction: but the optical law is subverted by the created optical fact.

The module with its gently swelling surface giving, not given by, the precise geometric sections, is in itself a model of entasis. Its expansiveness, as well as its geometric properties, explain both the apparent constancy of the sculpture's proportions and the quality of 'flow' up and down the *Column*.

Surprisingly, the most obvious positive-negative illusion, i.e. whether the element reads as convex or concave, does not present itself as a dominant and simple factor, but rather as the centre of a complex of ambiguities, which are both fused and set in motion by the internal modelling of the element. What has gained for the *Endless Column* its recent high esteem among artists – namely the idea of repetition – is seen in face of the object to be nothing in itself, unless the unit has a shape-potential that repetition will develop. What is involved at Tîrgu Jiu is not an escape from composition, but a daring and original re-statement of the antique but inescapable problem of the part-whole, whole-part relation.

Certainly, as one explores the *Endless Column*, its character as a 'whole', as a complete and *finite* object, emerges as dominant. Its appearance undergoes continuous change as one changes one's position in relation to it. Its broadest aspect (its front?) is presented by the diagonal view, which is aligned along the main north-south, east-west axes of the park. From this view, if the light falls across the *Column* so that one side is in shadow, the near edge reads as such a precise vertical that it seems as though a division between light and dark had been painted on the sculpture. The insistence of this vertical is so strong that one comes to realize that in a sculpture which is a celebration of verticality there is not one vertical plane or edge above the lowest incomplete element. As one circles the sculpture, as one advances towards it or retreats from it, there is a continuous interplay also between one's knowledge of its physical substantiality and its appearance as silhouette. Here again the modelling of the unit induces the most remarkable illusions, transforming the sculpture, when seen at a distance, into a string of up-ended ellipses, and from certain angles closer in, to a fully modelled spiral. Where the sculpture reads dark against the bright sky, the form is flattened and the left- and right-hand profiles take on an independent graphic life.

At any hour of the day no two views of the sculpture from different points can ever yield precisely the same image. The complexity and variety of the *Column's* perceived existence stand in contrast to that perceptual immediacy and unity that distinguishes Brancusi's effort in sculpture up to that time, and point to a radically new role for sculpture, whose form and structure would be ordered not by reference to the external world, nor by the ideal and contained universe of 'the object', but by directly articulating the perception of the spectator, whose world the sculpture has entered. At Tîrgu Jiu, Brancusi takes as his model for this venture first an object of common use, *The Table*; then an element of architecture, *The Gate*; then a structure of pure and sublime decoration, without function or justification, the *Column*. The progress towards abstraction is ineluctable. If there is one piece in the history of modern sculpture which in every respect deserves the title 'masterpiece', it is surely the Tîrgu Jiu *Endless Column*.

8 Gravity

A sense of gravity, of a strong relation between the form of the object and the ground on which it lies, has been central to the most vital modern sculpture since Rodin. Gravity unites sculpture and spectator in a common dependence on and resistance to the pull of the earth. Materials and structure, volume and space, the unity and proportions of sculpture, do not speak for themselves but articulate a complex and profound sense of our own being in the world. Because the object is fixed and still, its 'life' consists in the evocation, remaking even, of our freedom to move, within the given terms of its own structure. A sense of gravity is the factor which mediates our visual perception of sculpture with our conceptual knowledge of its 'real' form. The life of sculpture has in fact always subsisted in this gap between the known and the perceived; it was the articulation of this gap by perspective which gave painting its three centuries of dominance over sculpture. But it was the great achievement of Rodin to have recovered this territory for sculpture, using the same vehicle as the Renaissance masters, the human figure, to realize within its own structure the essential duality of sculpture, its internal, physical, and its external, perceived nature.

Had the historical consequence of Rodin's work been the renewal of naturalism in sculpture, then surely the great variety of poses which he handed on might have become the repertory of the next generation. Only the *Age of Bronze* of his mature sculpture depends on an articulation of the classical and stereotyped pose of the Apollo Belvedere type; thereafter every figure is so posed as to articulate its *own* expressive purpose. But Rodin's underlying purpose was neither mere invention nor the mere naturalistic recording of the nude model in movement (after all, we are told Canova had models perform in the same way). The great figure sculptures, from *John the Baptist* onwards are not in general figures in violent movement; rather they are in a state of suspended movement. *The Walking Man* is the type of this kind of sculpture. The perceived illusion of movement is countered by the enormous physical stability of the pose, the spread, straight legs forming that most stable of forms, the isosceles triangle. For any human being to stand erect, to resist gravity, means a continual if imperceptible muscular effort; Rodin uses the figure to recapture this effort *in sculptural terms*.

145

140 AUGUSTE RODIN *Eve c.* 1880–81

141 AUGUSTE RODIN *Nude Balzac Study C c.* 1891–92

The most convincing figures are built up from the feet. The disproportionate mass of the feet emphasizes their role as a gravitational anchor, as matter coterminous with the ground; their position and relation determines that of the legs, and then, progressing upwards, those of the hips, shoulders, arms and head. Rodin seems sometimes to have built up his figures without armatures, working centrally around a core of hardened clay. Nothing could display more clearly his tremendous skill, his commitment to and understanding of clay, than his feeling for gravity in putting the structural role on to an essentially unstructural, inert material. The continuity of articulation from core to surface, from the ground upwards, through all the members, is evident not only in such beautiful pieces as the *Prodigal Son* and the *Crouching Woman* discussed earlier but in all his most complete and satisfying figures, which are as widely different in character as the *Eve* and the studies for *Burghers of Calais* and *Balzac*.

It is in the final form of the *Burghers* and the *Balzac*, Rodin's most achieved and original public sculptures, that the power of gravity as a structuring element is most distinctively realized. The need in both instances was for a sculpture whose overall shape would read at a distance, carrying the burden of expression in itself, rather than in the posture or gesture of the component figures. The conventional pyramid form of public monuments, while giving visual and physical stability to the sculpture, implied a total gravitational unreality for the figures that composed it. Rodin was dissatisfied with this solution, both because it was a completely exhausted device and because it was utterly unreal in terms of his conception of the duty of public art: the straightforward, truthful presentation of a simple and urgent moral message.

142 AUGUSTE RODIN *The Burghers of Calais* 1886–88

The regular rectangle enclosing the *Burghers of Calais*, with the heads of all the figures aligned along the upper horizontal, the feet demonstrably rooted on the level ground base, was embodied in Rodin's initial conception of the sculpture.[1] This is a formal innovation, in terms of the history of monumental sculpture; and at the same time it is both truthful, in terms of Rodin's avowed naturalism; and economically expressive, in that the general horizontal mass of the work, articulated by the repeated verticals and off-verticals of the figures, in itself communicates the muted drama and pathos of the depicted situation. Whereas the overall form is immensely stable, the stability of each of the figures is variously threatened. Even the four-square *Burgher with the Key* gives one the feeling that he is rocking back and forth on his feet. The light penetrates and eats into the spaces between the figures, and especially between the two main groups. Viewed from the right-hand end, the insistent repetition of three exactly parallel and diagonal lower legs counteracts the effect of the highly individual and exactly realized heads by affirming the role of the limbs, of twenty-four arms and legs, in a gravitationally and expressively unified structure. The *Burghers of Calais* is not, as is sometimes said, six separate statues: it is as architectural as Rodin was capable of being, and is beyond a doubt his finest public sculpture; the repeated internal verticals, the arches formed by raised and gesturing arms, evoke the Gothic cathedrals to which he was so attached.

Much of the naturalistic detail and apparently rhetorical gesture of the *Burghers* has been eliminated from the *Balzac*, and to its expressive cost. The heavier drapery of the later sculpture, concealing the braced internal structure of the figure in favour of the simple silhouette, sacrifices most of the tension characteristic of the preliminary nude studies. From certain views the distribution of mass in the draped *Balzac* is hard to square with the convincing anatomy one knows to exist beneath. However, it is perhaps niggardly to question the success of a sculpture in which Rodin was reaching out, extending himself, as never before. The effort towards a dramatic and generalized simplification of volume was a heroic one, but simply not within his talent to accomplish without a self-conscious and obtrusive theatricality. The concept of the figure as a single, virtually unmodulated vertical was to have a profound effect, notably on Brancusi. Moreover, the *Balzac* is *about* gravity – the upward thrust of the figure from the plainly-stated horizontal base, its stability again disturbed by the pull of the earth, as the top-heavy head merging with the shoulders loads the figure into its precarious backward tilt. The *Balzac* represents the point at which gravity changes from an attribute of the figure – as in the studies – into the subject of the sculpture itself.

These two master-images for public sculpture, the horizontal rectangular block and the inflected vertical monolith, were evidently present in Brancusi's mind some forty years after the *Balzac*, when he was planning the monumental group at Tîrgu Jiu. The *Gate of the Kiss* perhaps rivals not the *Gate of Hell*, but the *Burghers of Calais*, to whose frontal aspect its external proportions correspond. The *Gate* is still, if only in terms of its continuous decoration, a group of figures. Paradoxically, it emphasizes both the massiveness and the transparency of the rectangular motif. Its enormous stability, its sheer physical weight, is belied by the subordination of every element – the material, the proportions, the nature and depth of relief – to its intended function – *the gate*, to be passed through not primarily by the body but by the eye and the spirit.

The incorporation of the diagonal into the soaring vertical, with which Rodin struggled with but partial success in the *Balzac*, is achieved apparently without effort in the masterly design of the Tîrgu Jiu *Endless Column*. In both the *Gate* and the *Column* Brancusi achieves on the gigantic scale a perfect equilibrium at the point at which the sculpture meets the ground. The dangerous and unstable relation between object and base of many of the small sculptures – touching at a point on a curved surface, the finest of footings, even on an edge (as in the *Fish*) – is replaced in the *Gate* and the *Column* by an actual gravitational stability, while the image and proportions of each piece, perceived as it rises from eye level, appear to release the sculpture from the pull of the earth.

The fundamental role of gravity in the emergence of modern sculpture is nowhere more evident than in the sculpture of Degas. Here a liberated conception of the figure in sculpture opened up possibilities for the free articulation of volume that remained untapped until steel came into general use as the central medium of sculpture, and are even now by no means exhausted. Because of the secrecy which surrounded its making, the objectivity of perception, the formalized subject-matter, but intrinsically because of the perfectly balanced and ordered structure of volume, the sculpture of Degas retains a 'timeless' quality, outside of nineteenth-century naturalism or the conscious archaism of twentieth-century sculpture.

There seems to me no doubt that Degas' most substantial achievement rests in his sculpture. If one sets aside Rodin's heroic and public effort, apparent in every piece, to rescue and re-orient sculpture, then individual sculptures by Degas, considered beside comparable works of Rodin, time and again impress by a quieter but more profound ambition, a more original conception of what sculpture could be made to do, a tauter and more worked-out quality of formal invention.

Degas grew up in the shadow of Ingres, and remained isolated from Manet and the other Impressionists in his continued concern for the primacy of contour in the realization of depicted volume. Where Manet would quote from unfamiliar masters in a deliberate challenge to the academic canons of

144 Edgar Degas *After the Bath, Woman Drying Herself* c. 1885–1900

figure painting, and Monet, Pissarro and Renoir simply disowned the conventional ambitions of Salon painting, Degas alone felt compelled to take on and renew the fundamental components of Ingres' art – drawing, composition, perspective, defined subject-matter. The innovations that Degas certainly made in painting – the use of unusual models, attitudes and subjects, of photography and Japanese prints in composition, of unexpected viewpoints and light sources – are perhaps best seen as intellectual attempts to subvert a set of received conventions, without however the deep conviction shared by his contemporaries in the necessity of painting as a means of expression.

The one area in which Degas was prepared to take risks, to put his intellect and his inhibitions on one side and engage his feelings, was in the modelling of volume. Over the years he moved from conventional oil painting into pastel and other more tactile techniques, affirming the figure and conventionalizing the background, in a progressive attempt to accommodate this ambition on the flat surface, and still within the general confines of the Ingres tradition, however liberated the colour or handling. But he must finally have come to realize the impossibility of this task, and acknowledge that, for his talent at that moment in history, sculpture was the only medium.

He had in fact been making sculpture ever since 1865; and 'as early as 1880 he devoted as much time to modelling as to painting',[2] although as he never considered himself a sculptor he never acquired even the rudiments of technique. In sculpture his lack of conventional training was to his profound advantage. What he lacked in elementary practical ability he more than compensated for in his freedom from the conventions that weighed on him so heavily in painting. His first free-standing sculptures, of horses, have a liveliness and freshness, both of observation and handling, possibly unequalled in European sculpture. Those elements which despite all efforts remained awkwardly separate in his painting – drawing, handling, composition, subject-matter – cohered and merged into one simple and direct physical activity. Colour, lighting, viewpoint – factors forced or theatrical in the paintings or pastels – are no longer an issue. New factors emerge – of real and illusioned balance in relation to gravity, of the continuously changing relation of real volumes when seen from every angle. Degas' sculpture is a triumph of *drawing*, not as design, but as the hard-won equilibrium of volume, surface and silhouette.

The poses of Degas' figures, women in the formalized postures of the dance or the toilet, take on a formal significance in the sculpture more substantial than the literary 'naturalism' of the figures as subject-matter in the painting. Even more than in Rodin, the variety and originality of Degas' figures underline the poverty of invention in European sculpture since the Renaissance, with its dependence on some half-dozen classical stereotypes.

145, 146 EDGAR DEGAS *Horse Clearing an Obstacle* 1865–81

147 AUGUSTE RODIN *Meditation* 1885

148, 149 EDGAR DEGAS *Dancer looking at the Sole of her Right Foot* 1896–1911

In sculptural terms, Degas' conception of the figure was more original than that of Rodin. The power of almost all Rodin's figures (after the *Age of Bronze*, whose attitude is classically derived) depends on a certain impression of incompleteness, even where the figure is physically complete, as though it had been torn out of some larger architectural or decorative context, its posture still implying a former and different function. If one considers, for example, the great number of figures, from the *Adam* onwards, whose heads are so unnaturally bowed that head, neck, shoulders, and sometimes raised arms form a continuous horizontal top profile, the suggestion of the caryatid form, of a given architectural function isolated from its context, is irresistible. Rodin's experience of architectural and decorative sculpture as a young man must have suggested to him a possible and expressive 'completeness' for the isolated figure, preserving its gravitational stability while implying an imbalance, an extension beyond its own physical limits, that was to characterize the fragments he later exhibited as complete sculpture. The bulky muscularity of Rodin's preferred models (what Brancusi called 'beefsteak'), the restlessness of surfaces, the unrelieved dynamic of diagonal axes, also affirm an ancestry in the Baroque. These obligations do not diminish Rodin's cultural achievement in returning health and confidence to sculpture, but they do point to the total and radical break with the past achieved by Degas' more modest and apparently less ambitious sculptural œuvre.

Attempts have been made to find precedents for the attitudes of Degas' models – for example Daumier's *Ratapoil* for the *Petite Danseuse*[3] – but the effort is misplaced. The pose, for example, of the *Dancer Looking at the Sole of her Right Foot*, not only has no ancestor in sculpture, but argues a conception of the figure as a balanced construct, a complete and satisfying organization of related volumes, that is as 'classical' as the perennial pose invented by the fifth-century Greek sculptors, in which the weight of the body is turned and shifted from one point to another in an ascending vertical from feet through knees, hips and shoulders. In the Degas sculpture, the figure is articulated, not as with Rodin from the ground upward, but from the pelvis outward, in every direction, thrusting and probing with volumes and axes until a balance is achieved. From what we know of Degas' methods – primitive and insubstantial armatures, modelling wax eked out with tallow and pieces of cork – an actual physical balance in the model was as much a consideration as the illusioned balance of the figure.

The effect of suspension in time and space, suspended action and suspended mass, challenging and teasing gravity, structure appearing to generate itself in mid-air, inevitably recalls the frequent use of this type of articulation by David Smith; more so, because of the identification of structure with material, than in the consciously Degaesque *Dancers* of González, where it is the *imagery* that is being followed, well within the limits of the material.

150 Julio González *Small Dancer* 1934–37

151 Edgar Degas *Dancer Putting on her Stocking* 1896–1911

152 David Smith *Australia* 1951

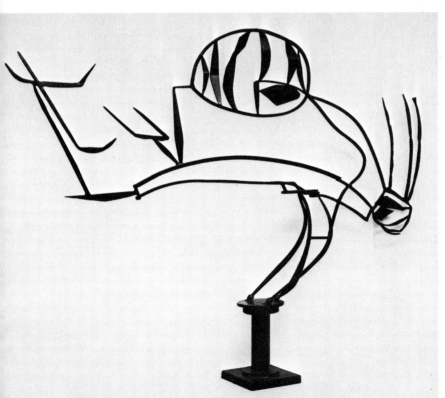

Smith stretches steel, stresses its junctions, takes balance to its limits, just as Degas stretched and stressed the human body in attitudes that were *in themselves structures* before work on the sculpture was started. The use of dancers as models ensured an elasticity of posture and a stamina in sustaining it beyond the reach of Rodin or of previous sculpture; but one senses that Degas' interest in the figure was essentially formal and abstract: performance was to him only the means of achieving the contained and tensioned equilibrium of form he desired.

It is notable that Degas' sculptures lose force when they stop short of, or exceed, the limits of the single, unsupported nude figure. The *Torso of Woman Sponging her Back*, evidently an intentional rather than accidental fragment, is unsatisfying without the extended limbs and head, demonstrating how essential to the reading of the tense and unfamiliar posture, the sense

153 EDGAR DEGAS *Torso of Woman Sponging her Back* 1896–1911

154 EDGAR DEGAS *The Masseuse* 1896–1911

of balance and distributed weight, is the delineation of every element in the structure. The distinction is evident here between the character of Rodin's modelling and that of Degas. In Rodin's fragments, modelling and articulation, surface and structure, are identified: the drama, the event, is *in* the surface, even the smallest area of it; thus the extension or curtailment of the fragment to include more or less of the subject is not crucial, and Rodin could add or subtract heads and limbs to different torsos, radically alter the fragment's orientation in space, without being disturbed by resultant incongruities. For Degas, modelling is subordinate to structure: the 'freedom' of handling of many of the figures has meaning only in the clearer reading of the *total* structure, causing the eye to register transition of volume in relation to the whole, rather than focus on local muscular detail.

Again, those figures which are part of a larger ensemble, such as the *Woman Washing her Left Leg*, seem pictorial, even anecdotal. The tension of the internal structure of the figure is drained off by the detail of the surrounding tableau, the modelling of which lacks the definition and urgency demanded by the figure. Much has been made of Degas' use of ready-made elements, such as the tub in this sculpture, or the clothing of the *Petite Danseuse*; but this seems a device of the order of those discussed in the painting, the novelty and immediacy of which ultimately reduce rather than enlarge the artist's freedom of action. The *Petite Danseuse* is itself a phenomenon, a freak: it must take its place beside Rodin's nude study for *Jean d'Aire* as a masterpiece of the cul-de-sac of total naturalism, of the unbelievably and monstrously lifelike. In spite of its modest proportions, it is, and was intended to be, the most spectacular and shocking sculpture of the nineteenth century, a triumph of inverted academicism; it indicates also Degas' intellectual kinship with later practitioners of the same genre, Duchamp and Giacometti.

But the *Petite Danseuse* is not among Degas' best sculptures, which are distinguished from practically all modern sculpture of the first rank, excepting possibly that of Matisse, by a genuine and intrinsic privateness. They were made to impress no one: Degas himself was satisfied with perhaps only the three which he had cast, *into plaster*, in his lifetime. So much for permanence! But it is in those few fragile wax models which by circumstance were preserved that the central quality of modern sculpture was distilled before history was ready for it. As for Degas' notorious aversion to emotion, there is more pathos, more heroism even, in his use of the human figure to express, through its own stressed posture, the 'grimace of the body',[4] an enduring and poised resistance to gravity, than in all the histrionics of Romantic art, Rodin included.

155 EDGAR DEGAS *Petite danseuse de quatorze ans* (*14-year-old Dancer*) c. 1880

Notes on the Text

Introduction (pp. 9–13)

1 Rainer Maria Rilke, *Rodin*, translated by Jessie Lamont and Hans Trausil, London 1949, p. 9.

2 From Rilke's diary for autumn 1900, quoted by Eudo C. Mason, *Rilke*, Edinburgh and London 1963, p. 47. See ibid., pp. 47–49, a discussion of Rilke's ideas at this period: 'he sees in sculpture, especially in Rodin's sculpture, the ideal type of the work of art altogether as he wants to realize it in his own poetry, and one of the essential points about this ideal is that the work of art should be cut off by a non-conducting vacuum from the ordinary give-and-take of human life'. See also Geoffrey H. Hartman, *The Unmediated Vision*, New York 1966, p. 86.

3 Brancusi in fact made the journey by train to Munich, possibly intending to stay there; and subsequently went on foot, taking jobs on the way, through Switzerland and into France as far as Langres, a distance of some 500 miles. Ionel Jianou, *Brancusi*, London· 1963, p. 30.

4 So designated in the catalogue to the Arts Council exhibition 'Rodin', London 1970, p. 63: 'the definitive form of the body beneath the robe (of the final Balzac figure)'.

5 Bronze no. 33, no. xxviii in John Rewald's critical catalogue, *Degas Sculpture*, London 1957.

6 Paul Valéry, *Degas, Manet and Morisot*, translated by David Paul, London 1960, p. 54.

7 Rilke, *Rodin*, p. 16.

1 Rodin (pp. 15–40)

1 For a detailed comparative account of the emergence of the Impressionist painters, see John Rewald's classic *The History of Impressionism*, New York 1946.

2 The traditional components of Rodin's thinking, his conception of the moral and public function of sculpture, are discussed at length in Albert Elsen, *Rodin*, New York 1963, pp. 13–19.

3 Dujardin-Beaumetz, 'Rodin's Reflections on Art', in Albert Elsen, ed., *Auguste Rodin, Readings on his Life and Work*, Englewood Cliffs 1965, p. 145.

4 Rainer Maria Rilke, *Rodin*, London 1949, p. 10.

5 Ibid., p. 16.

6 For Rodin's explanation of his contour method, see Dujardin-Beaumetz, in Elsen, ed., *Auguste Rodin, Readings . . .*, pp. 155–60.

7 'This is traditionally regarded as a study for the St John the Baptist, and dated accordingly 1877–78. However, the work was first exhibited in 1900, and it has been argued that the torso and legs were not joined until that time.

The torso appears to have been made in imitation of antique models, whereas the legs are taken from life.' Catalogue of Hayward Gallery exhibition 'Rodin', London 1970, p. 27.

8 Rodin's fragments, and his use of them in constructing figures, are well described in Leo Steinberg, *Other Criteria*, New York 1972, pp. 361–82.

9 'Rodin speaks of Barye as the master of masters. . . . Rodin thinks that Rude should be placed next to Barye, and then Carpeaux.' T. H. Bartlett, 'Auguste Rodin, Sculptor' (1889), in Elsen, ed., *Auguste Rodin, Readings. . .*, p. 92.

10 Quoted by J. B. Leishman in his introduction to *Rilke, Selected Poems*, Harmondsworth 1964.

11 Elsen, *Rodin*, p. 22.

12 Ibid., pp. 49, 67–68.

2 Brancusi: the Elements of Sculpture (pp. 41–58)

1 Ionel Jianou, *Brancusi*, London 1963, gives a vivid and apparently quite accurate account of Brancusi's childhood and schooling in Romania, pp. 22–28.

2 Sidney Geist, *Brancusi, a Study of the Sculpture*, New York and London 1968, the solid and by now surely the standard work on Brancusi, disentangles the confused chronology of the early years in Paris, pp. 17–24.

3 Elsen quotes Bourdelle, attempting, around 1900, to 'separate from Rodin'. He had come to dislike Rodin's 'too easily imitable tragically agitated faces, and holes in the planes of the flesh . . . [he] escaped from the hole, the accidental plane, in order to find the permanent planes'. Albert E. Elsen, *The Sculpture of Henri Matisse*, New York 1972, p. 43.

4 Brancusi's first direct stone-carving was the elongated, concave-fronted

Head of a Girl, influential on Modigliani, and now lost. Geist, *Brancusi, a Study of the Sculpture*, p. 28.

5 Sidney Geist was the first to draw attention to these sculptures as a group; see his introduction to the catalogue of the Museum of Modern Art retrospective exhibition 'Constantin Brancusi 1876–1957', New York 1969, p. 22.

6 There are other anatomical improbabilities, too, deriving from the fact that the sculpture is at once a fully volumetric representation and a four-sided relief.

7 Geist, *Brancusi, a Study of the Sculpture*, p. 97, notes the metal dowel inserted into the marble block before carving: 'The tall monolithic Birds in Space are not only marvels of art and dazzling examples of craftsmanship, they are engineering feats whose tolerances are as small as those of the design.' See also Athena T. Spear, *Brancusi's Birds*, New York 1969, pl. 43.

8 Geist, *Brancusi, a Study of the Sculpture*, p. 170.

9 Perhaps following the lead given by Werner Hofman, 'Über Matisse, Maillol und Brancusi', in *Museum und Kunst: Beiträge für Alfred Hentzen*, Hamburg 1970, pp. 97–108.

3 Picasso: Cubism and Construction (pp. 59–74)

1 Paul Valéry, *Degas, Manet and Morisot*, London 1960, p. 62.

2 *The Bottle* was Boccioni's only sculpture whose success and influence was commensurate with his inflated ambition: for a recent view of this flashy and academic talent see John Golding, *Boccioni's Unique Forms of Continuity in Space*, Newcastle upon Tyne 1973.

3 Neither could develop an impressive beginning. Duchamp-Villon, who might well have gone on to great things, died of typhoid contracted during military service in 1918, while Lipchitz's career from the early 1920s has been one of almost unimpeded degeneration into banal and regressive sentimentalism. For a detailed survey of the Cubist sculptors, see Douglas Cooper, *The Cubist Epoch*, London, Los Angeles and New York 1970, pp. 231–62.

4 See Clement Greenberg, 'Collage', in *Art and Culture*, Boston 1961 and London 1973, p. 70.

4 González (pp. 75–84)

1 Which makes it the more regrettable that González's sculpture is so often seen in the bronze casts made after the artist's death.

2 Smith generously acknowledged González in his rich and thoughtful article 'González: First Master of the Torch', in *Arts*, February 1956, pp. 34–37, 64–65.

5 Matisse (pp. 85–106)

1 As, for example, by Hilton Kramer in his perceptive and concise 'Matisse as a Sculptor' in *Bulletin*, Museum of Fine Arts, Boston, vol. LXIV, no. 336, 1966.

2 Quoted in Jean Guichard-Meili, *Matisse*, London and New York 1967, p. 168.

3 Matisse, comparing his ideal of sculpture with that of Rodin; quoted by Albert Elsen, *The Sculpture of Henri Matisse*, New York 1972, p. 43.

4 Elsen effectively compares Matisse's *Olga* (1910) with Maillol's *Méditerranée* (1905), Matisse's *Torso without Arms or Legs* (1909) with Maillol's *Ile de France*

(1909 or 1910): *The Sculpture of Henri Matisse*, pp. 98–99, 110–11.

5 The model for *The Serpentine* was a photograph in a book called *Mes Modèles*. I happened on this intriguing discovery in conversation with Mme Marguerite Duthuit, Matisse's daughter, in 1969. The original photograph is reproduced by Elsen, *The Sculpture of Henri Matisse*, p. 93.

6 Writing in 1969, I noted 'a kind of reverse perspective' as the active proportional device at work in this sculpture, in the context of a description of how the distortions of the figure Matisse arrived at in painting were fed into the the sculpture, then back into the painting. Elsen contests this view, citing Steichen's photograph of Matisse at work on *The Serpentine* as evidence that Matisse originally 'had probably been close to the model's proportions if not totally true to them'. In fact the photograph reveals the work in progress as much closer in rhythm and proportion to the final sculpture than to the original plump and inertly posed model. The eventual and decisive 'thinning and composing of forms' (Matisse's phrase) would only have been possible within a figure that already represented a considerable re-thinking of the motif. See Elsen, *The Sculpture of Henri Matisse*, pp. 91–93, and William Tucker, 'The Sculpture of Matisse', *Studio International*, July–August 1969, pp. 25–27 (reprinted from the catalogue to the exhibition of Matisse sculpture at the Victor Waddington Gallery, London 1969).

6 The Object (pp. 107–128)

1 The various overlapping meanings I have assigned to the words 'object' and 'objective' in this chapter may perhaps

be clarified by reference to Hannah Arendt, *The Human Condition*, New York 1959, pp. 120–22, 146–53.

2 I have deliberately emphasized Brancusi's relation to Rodin; clearly there were more immediate influences on the younger sculptor. Brancusi must especially have responded to Medardo Rosso: his subject-matter (women and children); the effect of pathos; the absorption of the features into the surface of the head. But Brancusi's sure and robust feeling for volume sets his sculpture apart from Rosso's fragile shells with their single, privileged view.

3 Excluding the *Table of Silence* at Tîrgu Jiu, which occupies an uneasy position between sculpture and use-object; see Chapter 7.

4 Quoted in the catalogue of the Moderna Museet exhibition 'Vladimir Tatlin', Stockholm 1968, p. 78.

5 Ibid., p. 76.

6 Quoted in the catalogue of the Stedelijk Museum and Hayward Gallery exhibition 'G. T. Rietveld, Architect', Amsterdam and London 1971–2, items 11–12 (unpaged).

7 This view is confirmed by Paul Overy, *De Stijl*, London and New York 1969, p. 127 and passim.

7 Brancusi at Tîrgu Jiu (pp. 129–143)

1 The column is inclined at 7° from the vertical. The cause of this is a subject for speculation. The column is made of cast-iron 'beads' threaded over a steel core, which was solidly rooted in concrete. The original finish was of molten brass sprayed on to the surface; this did not last, and the sculpture was painted in 1967 with bronze paint, and has probably been repainted since. For this and other valuable information on the Tîrgu Jiu ensemble, I am indebted to Sidney Geist, in a letter of August 1972.

2 'The Temple designed by Brancusi consists of only one room. In the middle there was to be a mirror of water, with the sculptures arranged about it. This room was to be reached through an underground passage. There were to be no doors or windows, merely an opening in the ceiling, specially designed as the sun moved across the sky so that its rays struck each of the five Birds in turn as they stood reflected in the water.' Ionel Jianou, *Brancusi*, London 1963, p. 56.

3 'The actual impossibility of *using* the Table and stools forces contemplation of them as design, and makes me think the arrangement is as Brancusi intended it. There is a photo with the stools up close, and people sitting on them – but *sideways* because their legs could not get under the table. The photo Brancusi gave Malvina Hoffman in 1938, before going off to Romania for the inauguration ceremonies, shows the stools two by two, but at a greater than practical distance from the table. The Table looks perilously like a table and of course exactly like Brancusi's studio furniture. What a problem – to make a table that isn't a table!' Geist, letter of August 1972.

I have seen examples of the same fundamental design – a round table surrounded by round stools – though of quite different proportions, by the roadside elsewhere in Romania.

4 See Sidney Geist, *Brancusi, a Study of the Sculpture*, New York and London 1968, p. 123.

5 Ibid., pp. 124–25.

8 Gravity (pp. 145–159)

1 There is a detailed description of the circumstances surrounding this com-

mission in Albert Elsen, *Rodin*, New York 1963, pp. 70–87.

2 John Rewald, *Degas Sculpture*, London 1957, p. 10.

3 Indicated by Charles Millard, in a lecture at St Martin's School of Art, London, November 1972.

4 'The more or less distorted bodies whose articulated structure he always arranges in very precarious attitudes . . . make the whole structural mechanism of a living being seem to grimace like a face'. Paul Valéry, *Degas, Manet and Morisot*, London 1960, p. 54.

Photographic Credits

Archives Photographiques, 7. Constantin Brancusi, 108. Bulloz, 142. Barney Burstein, 120. A. C. Cooper, 50. Courtesy Madame Georges Duthuit, 93, 101, 102, 103, 104, 106. Galerie de France, Paris, 72, 73. Dan Grigorescu, 131. Solomon R. Guggenheim Museum, New York, 109, 110. Galerie Louise Leiris, Paris, 52. Mansell-Alinari, 12. Leonard von Matt, 2, 145, 146, 148, 149, 151, 154. George Serban, 111. SCR, 82, 83. © by Spadem, Paris, 1973, 51, 58, 59, 60, 61, 62, 63, 64, 65. Nationalmuseum, Stockholm, 123, 124, 125. Rodney Todd-White, 21. Victoria and Albert Museum, London, 11. Courtesy Victor Waddington, 76, 77, 78, 79, 89, 94. John Webb, 1, 15, 20. Adam Woolfitt, 33, 132, 133, 135, 137, 139.

List of Illustrations

The dimension given for each sculpture is height, except where otherwise indicated. Measurements in inches or feet and inches (with centimetres in parentheses).

BRANCUSI, CONSTANTIN
(1876–1957)

4 *The Prayer*, 1907. Bronze, $43\frac{7}{8}$ (111·5). Muzeul de Artă, Craiova.

5 *The Kiss*, 1907. Stone, 11 (28). Muzeul de Artă, Craiova.

34 *Ecorché*, 1902. Painted plaster, $69\frac{1}{2}$ (177). Muzeul de Artă, Craiova.

35 *Pride*, 1905. Bronze, 12 (30·5). Muzeul de Artă, Craiova.

36 *Mlle Pogany*, 1912. Marble, $17\frac{1}{2}$ (44·5). Philadelphia Museum of Art.

37 *The Kiss*, 1911 (?). Stone, 23 (58·5). Philadelphia Museum of Art, Louise and Walter Arensberg Collection.

38 *Timidity*, 1915. Stone, $10\frac{5}{8}$ (27). Musée National d'Art Moderne, Paris, Brancusi Studio.

39 *Sleeping Muse*, 1909–11. Marble, 7 (17·8). The Hirshhorn Museum and Sculpture Garden, Smithsonian Institution, Washington, D.C.

40 *Prometheus*, 1911. Marble, length 7 (17·8). Philadelphia Museum of Art, Louise and Walter Arensberg Collection.

41 *Prometheus*, 1911. Bronze, length 7 (17·8). Collection Mrs Howard M. Kinney, Washington, D.C.

42 *Măiastră*, 1912. Brass, 24 (61); sandstone stand $11\frac{7}{8}$ (30·1). Collection of Mr and Mrs John Cowles, Minneapolis, Minnesota.

43 *Bird in Space*, 1941. Polished bronze, $76\frac{1}{8}$ (194·5). Musée National d'Art Moderne, Paris.

44 *The Prodigal Son*, 1915. Oak, $17\frac{1}{2}$ (44·5). Philadelphia Museum of Art, Louise and Walter Arensberg Collection.

45 *The Sorceress*, 1916. Wood, $39\frac{3}{8}$ (100). Solomon R. Guggenheim Museum, New York.

46 *Adam and Eve*, 1921. Oak, chestnut, limestone, $94\frac{1}{4}$ (299·4). Solomon R. Guggenheim Museum, New York.

47 *Torso of a Young Man*, 1916. Maple (stone base), 19 (48·5). Philadelphia Museum of Art, Louise and Walter Arensberg Collection.

48 *The Turtle*, 1943. Plaster, 9 (22·9). Musée National d'Art Moderne, Paris.

49 *The Cock*, 1924. Walnut, $36\frac{1}{8}$ (91·8); base $12\frac{1}{2}$ (31·8). Collection The Museum of Modern Art, New York. Gift of L. W. Berdeau.

50 *Fish*, 1926. Polished bronze, 5 (12·7). Private Collection.

108 *Torment I*, 1906. Plaster, $14\frac{1}{4}$ (36·2). Collection Mrs Zoe Dimitricu Busuleuga, Bucharest.

109 *Torment II*, 1907. Bronze, $11\frac{1}{2}$ (29·2). Collection Mr and Mrs Richard Davis, London.

110 *Sleeping Child*, 1908. Bronze, length $6\frac{1}{4}$ (15·9). From the private collection of Mr and Mrs Malcolm C. Eisenberg, Philadelphia, Pennsylvania.

111 *Sleep*, 1908. Marble, $10\frac{1}{4}$ (26·2). Muzeul de Arta R.S.R., Bucharest.

113 *Sleeping Muse*, 1910. Bronze, length 11 (28). Art Institute of Chicago, Arthur Jerome Eddy Memorial.

114 *Beginning of the World*, 1924. Polished bronze, on polished metal dish, length $10\frac{5}{8}$ (27). Musée National d'Art Moderne, Paris, Brancusi Studio.

115 *Cup I*, c.1918. Wood, $6\frac{1}{4}$ (16). Musée National d'Art Moderne, Paris, Brancusi Studio.

116 *Cup II*, c.1918. Wood, $7\frac{1}{2}$ (19). Musée National d'Art Moderne, Paris, Brancusi Studio.

117 *Cup III*, 1918–20. Wood, 9 (23). Musée National d'Art Moderne, Paris, Brancusi Studio.

118 *Cup IV*, before 1925. Wood, $10\frac{1}{4}$ (26). Musée National d'Art Moderne, Paris, Brancusi Studio.

131 *Endless Column* (detail of 137).

132 *Table of Silence*, 1937. Stone, table $31\frac{1}{2}$ (80), stools $21\frac{5}{8}$ (55), diam. of installation 18 ft 3 (556). Public Park, Tîrgu Jiu, Romania.

133 *Stools*, 1937. Stone. Public Park, Tîrgu Jiu, Romania.

134 *Leda*, 1923. Marble on stone base, 21 (53·4). Courtesy Art Institute of Chicago, bequest of Katherine S. Dreier.

135 *Gate of the Kiss*, 1937. Stone, 17 ft $3\frac{1}{2}$ (527). Public Park, Tîrgu Jiu, Romania.

136 *Study for Endless Column*, c.1936. Plaster, 19 ft $9\frac{1}{2}$ (603). Musée National d'Art Moderne, Paris, Brancusi Studio.

137–38 *Endless Column*, 1937. Cast iron, 96 ft 3 (2935). Public Park, Tirgu Jiu, Romania.

BRAQUE, GEORGES (1882–1963)

54 *Still-Life with Fish*, c.1909–11. Oil on canvas, $24\frac{1}{4} \times 29\frac{1}{2}$ (61·5 × 75). Tate Gallery, London.

CANOVA, ANTONIO (1757–1822)

8 *Study for Cupid and Psyche*, 1793. Clay, $9\frac{7}{8}$ (25). Museo Civico, Venice.

CÉZANNE, PAUL (1839–1906)

53 *Rocky Landscape, Aix*, 1885. Oil, $25 \times 31\frac{1}{4}$ (63·5 × 79·4). National Gallery, London.

DEGAS, EDGAR (1834–1917)

2 *Dancer Fastening the String of her Tights*, 1882–95. Bronze, $16\frac{3}{4}$ (42·5).

144 *After the Bath, Woman Drying Herself*, c.1885–1900. Pastel, $40\frac{7}{8} \times 38\frac{3}{4}$ (103·5 × 98·4). National Gallery, London.

145–46 *Horse Clearing an Obstacle*, 1865–81. Bronze, $11\frac{1}{4}$ (28·5).

148–49 *Dancer Looking at the Sole of her Right Foot*, 1896–1911. Bronze, $19\frac{1}{8}$ (49·5).

151 *Dancer Putting on her Stocking*, 1896–1911. Bronze, $18\frac{1}{4}$ (46).

153 *Torso of Woman Sponging her Back*, 1896–1911. Bronze, $19\frac{1}{4}$ (48·5).

154 *The Masseuse*, 1896–1911. Bronze, $16\frac{1}{4}$ (41).

155 *Petite danseuse de quatorze ans* (14-year-old Dancer), c.1880. Bronze, 39 (99). Tate Gallery, London.

DUCHAMP, MARCEL (1887–1968)

119 *In Advance of the Broken Arm*, 1915 (replica 1945). Readymade, 47¾ (121). Yale University Art Gallery, Gift of Miss Katherine S. Dreier.

120 *Fountain*, 1917 (replica 1951). Readymade, 14 (36). Collection Galleria Schwarz, Milan.

121 *Bottle Rack*, 1914 (replica 1964). Readymade, 25½ (64·2). Collection Galleria Schwarz, Milan.

122 *Hat Rack*, 1917 (replica 1964). Readymade, 9½ (23·5). Collection Galleria Schwarz, Milan.

GIACOMETTI, ALBERTO (1901–1966)

130 *Woman with her Throat Cut*, 1932. Bronze, 34⅝ (88). Collection Mr and Mrs Pierre Matisse.

GIBSON, JOHN (1790–1866)

11 *The Tinted Venus*, c.1850. Marble, 68 (173). Private Collection.

GONZÁLEZ, JULIO (1876–1942)

67 *Large Maternity*, 1930–33. Iron, 50 (127). Tate Gallery, London.

68 *Woman Combing her Hair*, 1933–36. Iron, 47½ (121). Moderna Museet, Stockholm.

69 *Small Head with a Triangle*, 1934–36. Silver, 9⅛ (23·1). Collection Hans Hartung, Paris.

70 *Gothic Man*, 1935. Iron, 20⅛ (51), base 2 (5). Collection Hans Hartung, Paris.

71 *Tunnel Head*, 1933–35. Bronze, 18¼ (46). Tate Gallery, London.

72 *Bust of a Woman*, c.1935–36. Iron, 19⅛ (48·4). Private Collection, Paris.

73 *Large Standing Figure*, c.1934. Bronze, 50⅝ (128·5). Private Collection.

150 *Small Dancer*, 1934–37. Silver, 8⅝ (22). Musée National d'Art Moderne, Paris.

GRIS, JUAN (1887–1927)

57 *The Teacups*, 1914. Oil, charcoal and pasted paper on canvas, 25½ × 36¼ (65 × 92). Kunstsammlung Nordrhein-Westfalen, Düsseldorf.

MANET, EDOUARD (1832–83)

7 *Olympia*, 1863. Oil on canvas, 51 × 73¼ (130 × 190). Louvre, Paris.

MATISSE, HENRI (1869–1954)

3 *The Serf*, 1900–03. Bronze, 36⅛ (91·8). The Baltimore Museum of Art, Cone Collection.

76 *The Jaguar, after Barye*, 1901. Bronze, 9 (22·9). Private Collection, Paris.

77–78 *Bust of an Old Woman*, 1900. Bronze, 24½ (62·3). Private Collection, Toronto.

79 *Ecorché*, 1902. Bronze, 9 (22·8). Private Collection, South Africa.

80 *Madeleine I*, 1901. Bronze, 23⅝ (60). The Baltimore Museum of Art, Cone Collection.

81 *Joy of Living*, 1905–06. Oil, 69 × 94 (175 × 240). The Barnes Foundation, Merion, Pennsylvania.

82 *The Dance*, 1910. Oil, $102\frac{3}{8} \times 129\frac{7}{8}$ (260 × 391). Hermitage, Leningrad.

83 *Music*, 1910. Oil, $102\frac{3}{8} \times 129\frac{1}{8}$ (260 × 389). Hermitage, Leningrad.

84 *Reclining Nude I*, 1907. Bronze, $13\frac{1}{2}$ (34·3). The Baltimore Museum of Art, Cone Collection.

85 *Two Negresses*, 1908. Bronze, $18\frac{1}{4}$ (46·3). The Hirshhorn Museum and Sculpture Garden, Smithsonian Institution, Washington, D.C.

86 *The Serpentine*, 1909. Bronze, 22 (56). The Royal Museum of Fine Arts, Copenhagen. Rump Collection.

87 *Head of Jeannette I*, 1910–13. Bronze, 13 (33). Collection Joseph H. Hirshhorn.

88 *Head of Jeannette II*, 1910–13. Bronze, $10\frac{3}{8}$ (26·5). Collection The Museum of Modern Art, New York. Gift of Sidney Janis.

89 *Head of Jeannette III*, 1910–13. Bronze, 24 (61). Private Collection.

90 *Head of Jeannette IV*, 1910–13. Bronze, $24\frac{1}{2}$ (62·3). Collection Joseph H. Hirshhorn.

91 *Head of Jeannette V*, 1910–13. Bronze, $22\frac{7}{8}$ (58). Collection The Museum of Modern Art, New York. Acquired through the Lillie P. Bliss Bequest.

92 *Henriette I*, 1925. Plaster, $11\frac{1}{2}$ (29·3). Collection Mr and Mrs Nathan Cummings.

93 *Henriette II*, 1927. Plaster, $12\frac{1}{2}$ (31·75). Private Collection.

94 *Henriette III*, 1929. Bronze, 16 (40·7). Waddington Galleries, London.

95 *Reclining Nude II*, 1927. Bronze, $11\frac{3}{4}$ (29·7). Tate Gallery, London.

96 *Reclining Nude III*, 1929. Bronze, $7\frac{7}{8}$ (20). The Baltimore Museum of Art, Cone Collection.

97 *The Back I*, c.1909. Bronze, $74\frac{3}{4}$ (190). Tate Gallery, London.

98 *The Back II*, c.1913–14. Bronze, $74\frac{1}{2}$ (189). Tate Gallery, London.

99 *The Back III*, c.1914. Bronze, 74 (188). Tate Gallery, London.

100 *The Back IV*, c.1929. Bronze, $74\frac{1}{2}$ (189). Tate Gallery, London.

101 *Seated Blue Nude I*, 1952. Paper cutout, $41\frac{3}{4} \times 28\frac{3}{8}$ (106 × 72). Private Collection.

102 *Seated Blue Nude II*, 1952. Paper cutout, $45\frac{3}{4} \times 35$ (116 × 88·9). Private Collection.

103 *Seated Blue Nude III*, 1952. Paper cutout, $45\frac{3}{4} \times 32\frac{1}{2}$ (116 × 82·7). Private Collection, Paris.

104 *Seated Blue Nude IV*, 1952. Paper cutout, $40\frac{1}{2} \times 29\frac{1}{8}$ (103 × 74). Private Collection.

105 *Armless and Headless Torso*, 1909. Bronze, $9\frac{3}{4}$ (24·7). Private Collection.

106 *Nude with Flowing Hair*, 1952. Paper cutout, $42\frac{1}{2} \times 31\frac{1}{2}$ (108 × 80). Private Collection, Paris.

MICHELANGELO BUONARROTI (1475–1564)

12 *The Dying Slave*, c.1573. Marble, $84\frac{5}{8}$ (215). Musée du Louvre, Paris.

PICASSO, PABLO (1881–1973)

51 *Musical Instrument*, 1914. Wood, partly painted, $25\frac{5}{8}$ (60). Private Collection.

52 *Houses on a Hill, Horta*, 1909. Oil on canvas, $25\frac{1}{2} \times 32\frac{1}{4}$ (65 × 81·5). Private Collection, Paris.

55 *Female Nude, Cadaqués*, 1910. Oil, $38\frac{3}{4} \times 30\frac{3}{8}$ (98 × 77). Philadelphia Museum of Art, Louise and Walter Arensberg Collection.

56 *Glass, Bottle and Guitar*, 1912. Collage, $18\frac{3}{4} \times 25\frac{5}{8}$ (46·5 × 62·5). Tate Gallery, London.

58 *Glass and Dice*, 1914. Painted wood, $9\frac{1}{4}$ (23·5). Picasso Collection.

59 *Guitar*, 1914. Painted metal, $37\frac{3}{8}$ (95). Picasso Collection.

60 *Glass, Pipe and Playing Card*, 1914. Painted wood and metal, diam. $13\frac{3}{8}$ (34). Picasso Collection.

61 *Still-life with Fringe*, 1914. Painted wood with fringe, 10 (25·5). Tate Gallery, London.

62 *Woman in Garden*, 1929–30. Bronze from original in iron, $82\frac{3}{4}$ (210). Picasso Collection.

63 *Construction in Wire*, 1930. Wire, $19\frac{5}{8}$ (50). Picasso Collection.

64 *Figure*, 1930–32. Iron, $31\frac{7}{8}$ (81). Picasso Collection.

65 *Woman's Head*, 1931. Iron painted white, $39\frac{3}{8}$ (100). Picasso Collection.

66 One of the introductory series of drawings in Balzac's *Le Chef-d'œuvre inconnu*, 1924. Pen, $11\frac{5}{8} \times 8\frac{3}{4}$ (29·6 × 22·4). Picasso Collection.

RIETVELD, GERRIT THOMAS (1888–1964)

126 *Red-Blue Chair (Unpainted)*, 1918. Wood. Collection Mrs P. van Noppen-Rietveld.

127 *Aluminium Chair*, 1942. Stedelijk Museum, Amsterdam.

128 *Chair with Leather Straps and Steel Frame*, 1927. Stedelijk Museum, Amsterdam.

129 *Plywood Chair*, 1927. Stedelijk Museum, Amsterdam.

RODIN, AUGUSTE (1840–1917)

1 *Nude Balzac Study F*, c.1896. Bronze, $37\frac{3}{4}$ (96). Musée Rodin, Paris.

6 *The Age of Bronze*, 1877. Bronze, 69 (175). Tate Gallery, London.

9 *Mask of the Man with the Broken Nose*, 1864. Bronze, $9\frac{1}{2}$ (24). Musée Rodin, Paris.

10 *The Man with the Broken Nose*, 1872. Marble, $22\frac{7}{8}$ (58). Musée Rodin, Paris.

13 *St John the Baptist*, 1878. Bronze, $78\frac{3}{4}$ (200). Tate Gallery, London.

14 *The Call to Arms*, 1878. Gilded bronze, $92\frac{1}{2}$ (235). Musée Rodin, Paris.

15 *Adam*, c.1880. Bronze, $75\frac{1}{2}$ (190). Musée Rodin, Paris.

16 *The Three Shades*, 1880. Plaster, $75\frac{5}{8}$ (192). Musée Rodin, Paris.

17 *Eternal Spring*, 1884. Marble, $26\frac{3}{4}$ (68). Musée Rodin, Paris.

18 *Crouching Woman*, 1880–82. Bronze, $37\frac{1}{2}$ (95). B. G. Cantor Art Foundation, California, on loan to the Art Institute of Chicago.

19 *The Prodigal Son*, 1889. Bronze, $55\frac{1}{8}$ (140). Musée Rodin, Paris.

20 *Study for Jean d'Aire*, c.1889. Bronze, 83 (210). Musée Rodin, Paris.

21 *Torso of Adèle*, c.1882. Bronze, 6 (15). William Shand Kydd, Esq.

22 *Torso of Seated Woman Clasping her Left Leg*, c.1890. Bronze, $13\frac{1}{2}$ (34). Collection Roland, Browse and Delbanco.

23 *Flying Figure*, 1890–91. Bronze, $8\frac{1}{4}$ (21). Musée Rodin, Paris.

24 *Iris, Messenger of the Gods*, 1890–91. Bronze, $37\frac{1}{2}$ (95). Collection Joseph H. Hirshhorn.

25 *Dance Movement A,* c.1910–11. Bronze, 28 (71). Musée Rodin, Paris.

26 *Dance Movement B,* c.1910–11. Bronze, 12¼ (31). Musée Rodin, Paris.

27 *Dance Movement C,* c.1910–11. Bronze, 13¾ (35). Musée Rodin, Paris.

28 *Dance Movement D,* c.1910–11. Bronze, 13¾ (35). Musée Rodin, Paris.

29 *Dance Movement E,* c.1910–11. Bronze, 14 (36). Musée Rodin, Paris.

30 *Dance Movement F,* c.1910–11. Bronze, 7 (18). Musée Rodin, Paris.

31 *Dance Movement G,* c.1910–11. Bronze, 12½ (32). Musée Rodin, Paris.

32 *Dance Movement H,* c.1910–11. Bronze, 11 (28). Musée Rodin, Paris.

107 *Large Head of Iris,* 1891. Bronze, 23½ (60). Tate Gallery, London.

112 *Aurora,* 1885. Marble, 22 (56). Musée Rodin, Paris.

139 *The Walking Man,* 1877. Bronze, 33¹⁄₁₆ (84·4). National Gallery of Art, Washington. Gift of Mrs John W. Simpson, 1942.

140 *Eve,* c.1880–81. Bronze, 67 (170). City of Manchester Art Galleries.

141 *Nude Balzac Study C,* c.1891–92. Bronze, 28¾ (73). Musée Rodin, Paris.

142 *The Burghers of Calais,* 1886–88. Bronze, 82⅝ (210).

143 *Monument to Balzac,* 1898. Bronze, 117 (300). National Gallery of Victoria, Melbourne.

147 *Meditation,* c.1896–97. Plaster, 55⅛ (140). Musée Rodin, Paris.

SMITH, DAVID (1906–1965)

74 *25 Planes,* 1958. Stainless steel, 136¾ (356). Private Collection, New York.

75 *Sentinel III,* 1957. Painted steel, 84 (213). Collection of Mr and Mrs Stephen D. Paine, Boston.

152 *Australia,* 1951. Steel, 79¾ (202). Collection, The Museum of Modern Art, New York. Gift of William S. Rubin.

TATLIN, VLADIMIR (1885–1953?)

123 *Corner Relief,* 1915. Iron, aluminium, zinc, presumed destroyed. Reconstruction made 1966[–70] by Martyn Chalk.

124 *Monument to the Third International,* 1919–20. Large scale model.

125 *Letatlin,* c.1932. Wood, silk and other materials.

Index

Italic figures refer to illustrations.